Themen 1

Lehrwerk für
Deutsch als Fremdsprache

Glossar
Deutsch-Englisch

bearbeitet von Alan G. Jones

Max Hueber Verlag

| 6. 5. | Die letzten Ziffern |
| 1992 91 90 | bezeichnen Zahl und Jahr des Druckes. |

Alle Drucke dieser Auflage können, da unverändert, nebeneinander benutzt werden.
1. Auflage
© 1984 Max Hueber Verlag · München
Umschlagillustration: Dieter Bonhorst · München
Gesamtherstellung: Pustet · Regensburg
Printed in the Federal Republic of Germany
ISBN 3–19–041371–1

Introduction

Dear student,

We hope that you will find the following materials of our German course "Themen" helpful for learning our language quickly and efficiently:

– course book (Kursbuch)
– cassette, with the texts from the Kursbuch
– workbook (Arbeitsbuch)
– listening comprehension programme (cassette and booklet)
– this glossary, with contrastive notes.

With the help of these materials – and of course with some effort on your part and some of your time! – you will be able, by the end of Book 2, to use German quite fluently in everyday situations.

"Themen" teaches you not only grammatical rules, but also how to use German correctly in everyday conversation. In other words, by the end of your course you will not just know German grammar, but will in fact be able to understand native speakers of German and to communicate with them in their language.

The three parts of "Themen" are designed to prepare you for the "Zertifikat Deutsch als Fremdsprache" (German as a Foreign Language Certificate) of the Goethe-Institut and the German Further Education Colleges' Association (end of Book 3) and for the "Grundbaustein Deutsch als Fremdsprache" (Basic Certificate in German as a Foreign Language) of the Further Education Colleges' Association (end of Book 2).

Course book (Kursbuch)

The Kursbuch is the basic guide-line for your activities in class. Every unit (Lektion) consists of three parts, marked A, B and C respectively.

Picture collages, drawings and posters which introduce the topic of the Lektion. You should respond to these in German in any way you can – either in complete sentences or with single words.

Texts and exercises, systematically arranged in steps (B 1, B 2 etc.). These parts form the core of each Lektion.

C

Texts of a more literary kind. They are not part of the compulsory teaching material of the Lektion and can be omitted if you or your teacher so wish.

The table of contents on pages 5 and 6 of the Kursbuch lists, besides the topic and the grammar covered by each Lektion, the so-called "Sprechintentionen", i.e. the functions you can do with the words and phrases that are introduced in the Lektion, like "asking", "giving orders", "apologizing" or "greeting". You can refer back to this list and tell at a glance the main points of each Lektion.

The following symbols indicate the skills (e.g. reading, listening, speaking, writing) being practised.

You can read this text in the Kursbuch and listen to it on the cassette. In class or at home, listen to the whole text on the cassette several times before you read it in the book. Then listen to the sentences one at a time and repeat them, paying particular attention to pronunciation and intonation. It is important to listen to the text over and over again until you are familiar with it. Act it out with one or more fellow students, then choose and practise some of the variations from the dialogue boxes printed below each text. Finally, you can act out the text and your own variations in front of the class – without the book. These texts are intended for conversation practice, not for teaching grammar rules.

The cassette is intended not only for class but for home use as well. You will learn faster if you play these texts several times at home. It is a good exercise to write out your own dialogue variations, which your teacher can then correct.

Listening passages

These passages are intended for listening practice. Thus they are only recorded on tape and not printed in the book. The exercises in the book will help you check whether you have understood the main points.

Note: You do not have to understand every word, or even every sentence, of these listening passages. It is enough if you get the basic idea or the most important information. Remember that the German you will hear in actual use will usually not be simplified language. Even so, you will want to pick out the main points of what has been said. The listening passages in "Themen" will give you practice in doing just this.

In the reading passages, too, you will find new words and grammatical structures, and there will undoubtedly be sentences you don't understand. But you will find that you can grasp the most important information with the knowledge you already have, and that will usually be sufficient. (Even when you read in English you will often scan rather than read every word.)

Recap exercises

In these exercises various points of the language which have been practised separately in earlier exercises are combined to be practised together.

For an exercise with the symbol you will need writing paper.

This symbol directs you to a section of the grammar summary at the end of the Kursbuch. The summary provides, chapter by chapter, a systematic overview of the grammar taught in Book 1. You can look up particular problems and check the rules. If you have forgotten a grammar rule already dealt with, the indicator arrows in the margin of the grammar pages will refer you back to earlier grammar notes.

Also at the end of the book you will find an alphabetical word list which will enable you to locate the page on which a word occurred for the first time. It contains all the words you should be able to use, but it does not list those words in the reading and listening texts which are irrelevant for the basic message of these texts. Words in bold print are the ones required for the Basic Certificate (end of Book 2).

Workbook (Arbeitsbuch)

The Arbeitsbuch is intended for independent work in class or at home. It offers exercises using the most important words, expressions and grammatical structures from each Lektion. If you do all the exercises in the Arbeitsbuch, you can be sure that you have covered the main points of each Lektion.

At the end of each Lektion in the Arbeitsbuch is a magazine section with various original German texts. These can be looked at in class or read at home. Again, remember that you do not have to understand every word, but just get the central message. Reading these passages will give you an idea of how it feels to read authentic German texts.

There are two editions of the Arbeitsbuch: Inland (home edition, for use inside Germany) and Ausland (export edition, for use abroad). The exercises are the same in both editions, but the reading passages in the magazine section are different. The Arbeitsbuch Inland contains texts which are important for a longer stay in a German-speaking country, whereas the Arbeitsbuch Ausland will interest learners abroad.

The grammar exercises entitled "Ihre Grammatik" relate directly to the grammar summary in the Kursbuch, so that you can use the rules shown there.

A key to the exercises (at the end of the Arbeitsbuch) helps you to check your own work. If your German is already very good, you will notice that for some exercises several solutions are possible. In these cases, the solution given in the key is the one most closely related to the teaching point of the Lektion in the Kursbuch. The exercises are marked '■' in the key.

The exercises are arranged in sections. There are exercises to train and reinforce vocabulary (WS), for grammar practice (GR), to help you remember the meaning of phrases and expressions (BD) and for practice in written expression (SA). (The abbreviations used to indicate these correspond to the Geman terminology: WS = Wortschatz = vocabulary; GR = Grammatik = grammar; BD = Bedeutung = meaning; SA = schriftlicher Ausdruck = written expression.) At the same time, margin cross-references (e. g. B 1/2, B 2 or B 3) indicate the sections of the Kursbuch to which the exercises relate. These you will find useful if you want to revise particular teaching points or make up a lesson you have missed.

Glossary with contrastive notes

This glossary offers for each Lektion:

a) All words and expressions with translations which are introduced and practised in the Kursbuch (in oral and written exercises) for active use. These words you should learn and remember.
b) Words and expressions in the listening and reading passages which are necessary for an understanding of the basic message of these texts. These are words that you need to be able to recognize but not to use. They are words that usually occur in texts which you will hardly ever have to produce yourself, like newspaper articles or advertisements, or they are words and expressions which you will want to learn only at a more advanced stage. These words are printed in italics.
c) Additional notes on features of German which could cause particular problems for you as an English-speaking learner. You will find that they supplement the grammar summary at the end of the Kursbuch, which is where all major grammatical points are covered for all users.

More often than not, a word has more than one equivalent in a foreign language, but to avoid confusion we have given only the meaning appropriate to the context in the book. You will often find others in a good dictionary – but leave that until you know more German anyway! Sometimes the meaning is clear only within the context of a phrase. You

6

learn the word "wie" in the context "Wie heißen Sie?", which means "What's your name?". It is really impossible to give an equivalent for "wie" on its own, because apart from "what", "wie" can also mean "how", "as", "such as", "like", and even "when" – depending on the context. In such cases, the English translation will be replaced by an arrow indicating "see next phrase". Likewise, an upward-pointing arrow indicates "see previous phrase".

Learning tips

Finally, we'd like to give you a few tips on how to learn German most efficiently with "Themen".

1. General tips

a) In all learning, we make mistakes. This is true of language learning, too. People who are afraid of making mistakes, and therefore say less, will learn more slowly than those who keep on talking in spite of their mistakes.

b) You cannot learn to drive a car just by listening to the instructor; if you don't practise, you'll never get your driving licence. Similarly, you will never learn to use a language just by studying the grammar rules; practice in speaking, listening, reading and writing is essential.

c) During free conversation practice in class, do not expect your teacher to correct you all the time – constant correction would stifle the free flow of conversation. However, where the Arbeitsbuch exercises are concerned, correction will be much more effective because the teacher can see your mistakes and explain them to you.

d) Work regularly at home, because class time is usually not enough. The Arbeitsbuch and this glossary will help you with individual work.

e) Arrange regular times with a partner for learning German together.

2. Specific tips

A. Vocabulary

a) Learn words in context rather than by themselves. For every word you want to learn, make up one or two example sentences. Do this frequently.

b) Write out from each Lektion the words which you have learnt previously but have forgotten. Look them up in the alphabetical index and go back to the place where they first occurred. Then make up sentences containing these words.

c) Write out at least 15–20 sentences from the Kursbuch, leaving out one word in each sentence. Then fill in the missing words.

d) Make a card index. Fill in a card with each new word learnt, with the context but without the translation. Every two or three days, check which words you have forgotten, and put these cards into a separate box for special attention. Later, when you find you can remember the meaning of these words, return them to the main file.

B. Speaking

a) At home, make up variations on the basic dialogues. Write them out and ask your teacher to correct them for you. If you have a friend who is also learning German, act out together the dialogues in the Kursbuch and your own variations on them.

b) Listen to the dialogues on the cassette sentence by sentence and repeat each one. Do this several times in succession.

C. Listening

a) Listen to as much German as you can, even if you do not understand everything. This way you will get used to normal conversational speed and a genuine German accent. Even if you have the printed text available, you should listen without looking at it. You will find the special listening programme for "Themen" helpful to practise listening comprehension (cassette, Hueber reference no. 12.1371; booklet, Hueber no. 14.1371).

b) Write out in German the dialogues from the cassette, then check with the printed text to see if you heard correctly. Do not worry too much about spelling and punctuation; in this exercise, the object is to train your ear.

c) Make notes on a listening comprehension passage, and then write out a summary of what it says.

D. Reading

a) Read as much German as you can. At home, read through any texts from the Arbeitsbuch that you have not studied in class. Collect German texts.

b) Make notes about the main points of a passage, then write out a summary of it.

c) Practise at home with a partner from your class. Ask and answer questions about the text.

E. Writing

Make notes and then write a letter in German to a real or imaginary person (for example: you have moved to another town and want to tell a friend how to get there; you want to invite someone for a meal; you want to tell a friend what you did last week; you want to send greetings from a holiday . . .). You could ask your teacher to correct your work.

Lektion 1 Kursbuch

|

Guten Tag — Hello → see contrastive notes, p. 14
  Guten Tag, ich heiße Thomas Meier. — Hello, I'm Thomas Meier.; My name is …
ich — I → see contrastive notes, p. 14
heiße (→ heißen) — to be called ; to be named
Auf Wiedersehen — Goodbye
wie? — →
  Wie heißen Sie? — What's your name?
Sie — you → see contrastive notes, p. 14
mein — my
  Guten Tag, mein Name ist Luisa Tendera. — Hello, my name is Luise Tendera.
Name — name → see contrastive notes, p. 14
ist (→ sein) — is
bitte — →
  Wie bitte? — pardon?
verstehen — to understand
  Ich verstehe nicht. — I don't understand.
nicht — not
wer? — who?
  Wer ist das? — Who is that?
das — that
er — he
  Er heißt Jean Paul Faivre. — He's Jean Paul Faivre. ; His name is …

|

Entschuldigung — Excuse me ; I'm sorry
  Entschuldigung, sind Sie Herr Meier? — Excuse me, are you Mr. Meier?
sind (→ sein) — are
nein — no
  Nein, ich bin Peter Miller. — No, I'm Peter Miller.
bin (→ sein) — am
Herr — Mr.
  Entschuldigung, sind Sie Herr Meier? — Excuse me, are you Mr. Meier?
Frau — Mrs. → see contrastive notes, p. 14
Fräulein — Miss
Ja — Yes

| buchstabieren | to spell |
| Buchstabieren Sie bitte! | Please spell. |

und	and
Und ist das Frau Müller?	And is that Mrs. Müller?
Wie geht es Ihnen?	How are you?
danke	thank you
Danke, gut.	Thank you, fine.
gut	well
es geht	All right, not so bad.
so	so
Nicht so gut.	Not so well.
auch	→
Auch gut.	I'm well, too.

kommen	to come
Ich komme aus USA.	I come from the USA. ; I'm from the USA
aus	from
USA	USA
woher?	where from?
Und woher kommen Sie?	And where do you come from?
Deutschland	Germany
... aus Deutschland	... from Germany
Nordamerika	*North America*
Kanada	*Canada*
Südamerika	*South America*
Bolivien	*Bolivia*
Peru	*Peru*
Brasilien	*Brasil*
Argentinien	*Argentina*
Chile	*Chile*
Venezuela	*Venezuela*
Kolumbien	*Columbia*
Uruguay	*Uruguay*
Großbritannien	*Great Britain*
Schweiz	Switzerland
Afrika	*Africa*

Senegal	*Senegal*
Ägypten	*Egypt*
Elfenbeinküste	*Ivory Coast*
Zaire	*Zaire*
Tansania	*Tanzania*
Kenia	*Kenya*
Sudan	*Sudan*
Ghana	*Ghana*
Nigeria	*Nigeria*
Äthiopien	*Ethiopia*
Europa	*Europe*
Spanien	*Spain*
Österreich	Austria
Frankreich	*France*
Italien	*Italy*
Dänemark	*Denmark*
Türkei	*Turkey*
Ungarn	*Hungary*
Polen	*Poland*
Rumänien	*Romania*
Bundesrepublik Deutschland	Federal Republic of Germany (West Germany)
DDR (Deutsche Demokratische Republik)	GDR (German Democratic Republic, East Germany)
Belgien	*Belgium*
Niederlande	*Holland, Netherlands*
Griechenland	*Greece*
Schweden	*Sweden*
Norwegen	*Norway*
Finnland	*Finland*
Asien	*Asia*
Indien	*India*
Japan	*Japan*
China	*China*
Indonesien	*Indonesia*
Thailand	*Thailand*
Iran	*Iran*
Israel	*Israel*
Libanon	*Lebanon*
Australien	*Australia*
von	from
von der Elfenbeinküste	from the Ivory Coast

Seite 11 | Page 11

Guten Morgen.	Good morning.
Fisch	fish
Ach so.	Oh, I see.
Bach	stream ; brook ; creek
dann	then
Ja dann – . . .	Well then . . .
was?	what?
Was? Sie heißen Fisch?	What? Your name is Fisch?
warum?	why?
komisch	strange
Komisch – Sie heißen Bach?	Strange – your name is Bach?
denn	→ see contrastive notes, p. 23
Woher kommen Sie denn?	Where are you from?
Na so was!	Well I never!
Mond	moon
See	lake
Kuh	cow
Faß	barrel
Wein	wine
Berg	mountain

Seite 12 | Page 12

er	he
Er kommt aus der Bundesrepublik.	He comes from the Federal Republic.
sie (Sg.)	she → see contrastive notes, p. 14
Sie kommt aus Österreich.	She comes from Austria.
sie (Pl.)	they
Sie kommen aus USA.	They come from the USA.
weiß (→ wissen)	to know
Das weiß ich nicht.	I don't know.
Lösung	*solution*
Seite	*page*

Seite 13 | Page 13

Kurs	*course*
Institut für Deutsch als Fremdsprache.	*Institute for German as a Foreign Language*
Teilnehmerliste	*List of participants*
Raum	*room*
Vorname	*first name (Christian name)*

Land	*country*
Stadt	*town, city*
Tunesien	*Tunisia*
Korea	*Korea*
in	in
Er kommt aus Atlanta in USA.	He comes from Atlanta in the USA.
Marokko	*Morocco*
Kommt Lucienne Destrée aus Marokko?	Does Lucienne Destrée come from Morocco?

Seite 14   Page 14

da	→
Wer ist da bitte?	Who's speaking?
hier	→
Nein, hier ist . . .	No, this is . . .
Auf Wiederhören.	Goodbye. → see contrastive notes, p. 14
spielen	to play
Dialog	dialogue
Spielen Sie den Dialog.	Act out the dialogue.
anrufen	*to phone*

Seite 15   Page 15

wie viele?	how many?
Wie viele Wörter finden Sie?	How many words can you find?
Wort, Wörter (Pl.)	word, words
finden	to find
wieviel?	how much?
Wieviel ist das?	How much is that?
paßt (→ passen)	to fit
Was paßt nicht?	Which word does not fit?
du	you → see contrastive notes, p. 14
Woher kommst du?	Where do you come from?
hören	to hear, to listen to
Hören Sie den Dialog.	Listen to the dialogue.
beantworten	to answer
Beantworten Sie dann.	Then answer.

Hallo	*Hello*
Mein Gott	*Good heavens! My Goodness!*
oder	*or*
Oder bin ich . . .?	*Or am I . . .?*
vielleicht	*perhaps*
Bin ich vielleicht . . .?	*Could I be . . .? ; Could I perhaps be . . .?*

Contrastive notes

Guten Tag. (page 7): You can use *Guten Tag.* whenever either *Good morning!* or *Good afternoon!* would be appropriate. *Guten Morgen.* is used only in the morning.

Frau (page 8): Use *Frau* for any woman over 20, married or single.

Auf Wiederhören – Auf Wiedersehen (pages 14, 7): When speaking on the telephone, don't use *Auf Wiedersehen* (because you can't really see the person you are talking to). Instead, use *Auf Wiederhören.*

Sie (page 7), sie (page 12), du (page 15): Both *Sie* and *du* mean *you*. *Du* is used only for relatives, close friends, children and animals. When you are not sure which one to use, stick to *Sie* until the person you are talking to invites you to say *du*. Note that *Sie* is written with capital when it means *you*; with a small letter *sie* means *she* or *they*. *Du* is written with a small d, except in letters, where it takes the capital.

ich (page 7): *Ich* is always written with a small i, unless, of course, it starts a sentence.

Name (page 7): German uses capital letters for all nouns, even within a sentence.

Word order (page 124): In German, as in English, the words do not stand in the sentence in random sequence but hold specific positions, depending on the category of word they belong to or the function they have in the sentence. Accordingly, our grammar pages are coloured as follows:
Verb: tinted dark blue
Subjekt (subject): tinted yellow
Obligatorische Ergänzung ("compulsory supplement"): tinted light blue
Angabe ("additional information"): tinted green
The verb plays an important role in two ways: on the one hand it serves as a point of reference for the subject, which positions itself next to it, either preceeding or immediately following it, depending on whether the speaker wants to make a statement, ask a question

or give a command; on the other hand, each individual verb determines what kind of supplement – if any – is necessary for the completion of the sentence. In most cases, these "compulsory supplements" will appear obvious to you when you consider the meaning of a verb (for instance, you cannot make a complete statement using *ich heiße* without telling your name, which is indeed the "compulsory supplement" to the verb *heißen*), but you will probably come across a few instances where this inner logic will not be immediately clear to you.

In German this "compulsory supplement" is called "obligatorische Ergänzung". In our colour scheme, it takes on a light blue tint to show its close connection to the verb. All those parts of the sentence which are neither verb nor subject nor "compulsory supplement" (and whose omission would not touch on the <u>grammatical</u> completeness of the sentence) are "additional information" and belong in the green space under the heading "Angabe". Most often, this will be information concerning time, or modifiers like *bitte, denn, nicht* and others.

1a) Aussagesatz
In a statement, the subject precedes the verb.
Ich heiße Hans Müller.

1b) Satzfrage mit Inversion
In a question expecting the answer yes or no, the verb opens the sentence and is followed immediately by the subject.
Heißen Sie Hans Müller? Sind Sie Hans Müller?

1c) Imperativ mit Inversion
The same rule applies when giving a command or making a request.
Buchstabieren Sie bitte!

1d) Wortfrage mit Fragewort und Inversion
In questions with an interrogative *(wer?, wie?,* etc), the subject again moves to the position after the verb, thus inverting the standard word sequence. Therefore, such interrogatives can be seen as "inversion signals".
Wer ist das?
Wie heißen Sie?

Seite 17	Page 17
Bäcker	baker
Krankenschwester	nurse
Student	student
Mechaniker	mechanic
Bauer	farmer
Ingenieur	engineer
Programmierer	programmer
Graphikerin	commercial artist (f)

Seite 18	Page 18
von Beruf sein	→
Was sind Sie von Beruf?	What's your job?
Lehrer, Lehrerin	teacher (m; f) → see contrastive notes, p. 22
Ich bin Lehrerin.	I am a teacher.
Angestellter, Angestellte	white collar worker; employee (m; f)
die Berufe der Deutschen	*the Germans' occupations*
Kfz.-Mechaniker	*motor mechanic ; auto mechanic*
Maschinist	*machine operator*
Männer (Pl.)	*men*
Frauen (Pl.)	*women*
Maurer	*bricklayer*
Lagerist	*store keeper; warehouse clerk*
Groß-, Einzelhandelskaufmann	*wholesale or retail trader*
Unternehmer	*owner of a firm*
Elektriker	*electrician*
Landwirt, Landwirtin	*farmer (m; f)*
Bauer, Bäuerin	*farmer (m; f; colloq.)*
Techniker	*technician*
Kraftfahrer	*driver; chauffeur*
Polizisten (Pl.)	*policemen*
Soldaten (Pl.)	*soldiers*
Schlosser	*fitter; mechanic*
Büroangestellter, Büroangestellte	*office worker (m; f)*
Friseuse	*hairdresser (f)*
Hauswirtschafterin	*housekeeper*

Köchin	*cook (f)*
Buchhalterin	*book keeper; accountant (f)*
Sprechstundenhelferin	*doctor's or dentist's assistant (f)*
Näherin	*seamstress*
Warenprüferin	*checker; inspector (f)*
Packerin	*packer (f)*
Sekretärin	*secretary (f)*
Raumpflegerin	*cleaner; cleaning woman*
Verkäuferin	*sales girl*
alt	old
Wie alt ist er/sie?	How old is he/she?
wo?	where?
Wo wohnt er/sie?	Where does he/she live?
wohnen	to live

Seite 19	Page 19
Kaufmann	sales executive; commercial clerk
Sekretärin	secretary
Schlosser	fitter
Telefonistin	telephonist; switchboard operator
Guten Tag, ist hier noch frei?	Hello, can I sit here?
bitte	please
neu	new
Sind Sie neu hier?	Are you new here?
arbeiten	to work
Ja, ich arbeite hier erst drei Tage.	Yes, I have only been working here for three days.
erst	only → see contrastive notes, p. 22
Tag, Tage (Pl.)	day ; -s
machen	to do
Ach so, und was machen Sie?	I see, and what do you do?
Ich bin Mechaniker.	I am a mechanic.
	→ see contrastive notes, p. 23
übrigens	by the way
Übrigens: Ich heiße Jan v. Groot.	By the way, my name is Jan van Groot.
natürlich	of course
schon	already → see contrastive notes, p. 22
Nein, ich arbeite hier schon vier Monate.	No, I have already been working here for four months.
Monat, Monate (Pl.)	month ; -s

17

Leute (Pl.)	people
Deutsche	German (f)
Sie ist Deutsche.	She is German.
leben	to live
Sie lebt in Hamburg.	She lives in Hamburg.
verheiratet	married
Sie ist verheiratet.	She is married.
haben	to have
Sie hat zwei Kinder.	She has two children.
Kind, Kinder (Pl.)	child, children
sein, seine	his
Levent Ergök und seine Kollegen	Levent Ergök and his colleagues
Kollege, Kollegen (Pl.)	colleague; -s
Automechaniker	motor mechanic, auto mechanic
Er ist Automechaniker	He works as a motor mechanic
bei Mannesmann.	with Mannesmann.
bei	with, at
seit	since, for → see contrastive notes, p. 23
Er ist seit drei Jahren in	He has been in the
der Bundesrepublik Deutschland.	Federal Republic for three years.
Jahr, Jahre (Pl.)	year, years
denn	because, for, as
... denn Wohnen, Essen und Trinken	... because living, eating and drinking
sind teuer in Deutschland.	are expensive in Germany.
Essen	eating, food
Trinken	drinking
teuer	expensive
Schausteller	showman; a fairground entertainer
Peter-Maria Glück, Schausteller,	Peter-Maria Glück, showman,
wohnt im Wohnwagen.	lives in a caravan.
im (= in dem)	in the
Wohnwagen	caravan
heute	today
Er ist heute in Stuttgart, morgen in	Today he is in Stuttgart, tomorrow in
Heidelberg und übermorgen in Mann-	Heidelberg and the next day in Mannheim.
heim.	
morgen	tomorrow
übermorgen	the day after tomorrow
zusammen	together
Sie arbeiten zusammen in ...	They work together in ...
Ergänzen Sie!	Complete!

Wohnort	*place of residence*
Familienstand	*marital status*

Seite 21 | ## Page 21

studieren	*to study → see contrastive notes, p. 23*
Monika studiert Medizin.	*Monika is studying medicine.*
Medizin	*medicine*
Produktion	*production*
Sie arbeitet in der Produktion.	*She is working in the production department.*
leiten	*to lead*
Sie leitet eine Gruppe von 20 Männern.	*She leads a team of 20 men.*
eine Gruppe	*a team*
Mann, Männer (Pl.)	*man, men*
Chemiker	*chemist; expert in chemistry*
Er ist Chemiker.	*He is a chemist.*
ledig	*single*
Er ist ledig und wohnt allein.	*He is single and lives alone.*
allein	*alone*

Seite 22 | ## Page 22

Hallo	Hello → see contrastive notes, p. 22
Hallo, Ibrahim.	Hello, Ibrahim.
sagen	to say, to tell
Sag mal, was machst du denn hier?	Tell me, what are you doing here?
mal (= einmal)	just
du	you
denn	→ see contrastive notes, p. 23
lernen	to learn, to study
Ich lerne hier Deutsch.	I am learning German here.
Deutsch	German
möchte (→ mögen)	would like → see contrastive notes, p. 23
Ich möchte doch in Köln Chemie studieren.	I would like to study chemistry in Cologne, as you know.
doch	→ see contrastive notes, p. 23
Chemie	chemistry
studieren	to study
ach ja	oh yes
Ach ja, richtig.	Oh yes, that's right.
richtig	right, correct

sprechen	to speak
Sie sprechen aber gut Deutsch.	You speak German so well.
aber	but → see contrastive notes, p. 23
na ja	well
Na ja, es geht.	Well, it's okay.; Well, it's all right.
Bekannter, Bekannte (Pl.)	*acquaintance, -s*
Fremder, Fremde (Pl.)	*stranger, -s*
Freund, Freunde (Pl.)	*friend, -s*
Student, Stundenten (Pl.)	*student, -s*
Familie	*family*
Kind, Kinder (Pl.)	*child, children*

Seite 23   Page 23

Spanisch	Spanish
Packer	packer
Kauffrau	sales executive (f)

Seite 24   Page 24

Feuer,	a light
Hast du Feuer?	Have you got a light?
leider	unfortunately; I'm afraid not.
Nein, leider nicht.	No, I'm afraid not.
warten	to wait
Wartest du hier schon lange?	Have you been waiting here long?
lang, lange	long
Stunde, Stunden (Pl.)	hour, hours
Minute, Minuten (Pl.)	minute, minutes
liegen	→
Wo liegt das denn?	Where is that?
bei	near
bei Wien.	near Vienna.
Österreicher	Austrian
Ich bin Österreicher.	I am an Austrian.

Seite 25   Page 25

Italiener	Italian (man)
Italienerin	Italian (woman/girl)
italienisch	Italian (adjective)
Student	*student*

20

Kellner	*waiter*
falsch	wrong
Was ist hier falsch?	What's wrong here?
Elektrotechniker	*electrical engineer*
es gibt	there is → see contrastive notes, p. 23
Es gibt viel Arbeit in der Bundes- republik Deutschland	There is a lot of work in the F.R.G.
viel	much, a lot (of)
Arbeit	work

Seite 26   Page 26

Geburtstag	*date of birth*
Geburtsort	*place of birth*
Original	*original*
Fälschung	*falsification*
stimmt (→ stimmen)	correct
Was stimmt hier nicht?	What is not correct?

Seite 27   Page 27

Interviewspiel	*interview game*
fragen	*to ask*
Nachbar	*neighbour*
Fragen Sie Ihren Nachbarn!	*Ask your neighbour!*
Start	*start*
Land	*country*
Alter	*age*
Adresse	*address*
Sprache	*language*
Staatsangehörigkeit	*nationality*
Ziel	*goal*

Seite 28   Page 28

wissen von	to know about
Was wissen Sie von Nyerere?	What do you know about Nyerere?
Papst Johannes Paul II.	Pope John Paul II.
Tennisspieler	tennis player
Ordensschwester	nun
Politiker	politician
Schriftstellerin	writer (f)

berichten	→
Berichten Sie über ...	Give informations about ...
Personenraten	Guess who game
antworten	to answer
nur	only
Antworten Sie nur "ja" oder "nein".	Only answer "yes" or "no".
weiblich	female
männlich	male
Ist sie weiblich/männlich?	Is she female/male?
ledig	single
verheiratet	married
Ist er/sie ledig/verheiratet?	Is he/she single/married?

## Seite 29	## Page 29

weiß	*white*
schwarz	*black*
wohnhaft	*resident*
geboren	*born*
wann?	*when?*
Wann sind Sie geboren?	*When were you born?*
am	*on the*
Am 5. 5. 55	*on the 5th May 1955; May 5th 1955*
Ihre	*your*
Wie heißt Ihre Frau?	*What is your wife's name?*
geborene	*born, née*
Isolde Weiß – geborene Schwarz.	*Isolde Weiss – née Schwarz.*
also	*so*
schwarz arbeiten	*to be a moonlighter; to work on the sly*
verheiratet mit	*married to*
verboten	→
Das ist verboten.	*That's illegal.*

## Seite 30	## Page 30

Nichtstuer	*layabout; idler, loafer*
Das macht nichts.	*That doesn't matter.*
möglich	*possible*
Aber das ist leider nicht möglich.	*But unfortunately that's not possible.*
deshalb	*therefore*
Was heißt das auf deutsch?	*What is the German for ... ?*
	What is that in German?

Contrastive notes

Lehrerin, Studentin (page 18): Many words denoting professions or nationality add *-in* for the feminine form. For instance, a man is *ein Lehrer*, a woman is *eine Lehrerin*.

erst – schon (page 19): When referring to something that started in the past and is still going on, either *erst* or *schon* is used. Using *erst* indicates that something has been going on for only a short while, whereas *schon* means that it has been going on for quite some time.

Ich bin Mechaniker. (page 19): Note that in German you refer to somebody's profession without the indefinite article used in English. *Ich bin Mechaniker.* means *I am a mechanic.*

seit (page 20): Using *seit* indicates that something started at a particular moment in the past and is still going on. *Er ist seit drei Jahren in der Bundesrepublik.* means that he came three years ago and is still here. Unlike *erst* and *schon*, *seit* does not imply a subjective notion as to whether this duration should be considered short or long. To do this, you have to add *erst* or *schon: Er ist schon seit drei Jahren in der Bundesrepublik.*

studiert (page 21): In German, the distinction between *she studies* and *she is studying* is not made by different forms of the verb. Accordingly, there is only one form for the present tense.

Hallo! (page 22): *Hallo* is far more colloquial than *Guten Tag*. You can use it when you are on friendly and easy terms with someone.

denn (page 22): *Denn* can be used as a modifier in questions to stress that you have a personal interest in the answer.

doch (page 22): *Doch* has various meanings. In this case it is a modifier signalling that reference is made to something of common knowledge to the parties concerned, e. g. *Ich möchte doch in Köln Chemie studieren. – I want to study chemistry in Cologne, as you know.*

aber (page 22): In this case, *aber* is a modifier with an adjective and indicates surprise and/or admiration.

möchte (pages 22 and 127): *Möchte* means *would like* and can be combined, as in English, with any other verb in the infinitive form. Note that whenever two verbs are used in a sentence, the conjugated verb (in our case, *möchte*) occupies the first verb position (before or after the subject), whereas the verb in the infinitive form goes to the end of the sentence, which is the second verb position.

Ich möchte hier Deutsch lernen.
Möchten Sie auch in Paris wohnen?

es gibt (page 25): *Es gibt* is the German equivalent of both *there is* and *there are*.

23

Lektion 3 Kursbuch

Seite 31   Page 31

m^2 (der Quadratmeter)	m^2 (square metre)
das Kinderzimmer	children's room
das Zimmer	room
das Schlafzimmer	bedroom
das Bad	bathroom
das Dachgeschoß	attic, top floor
das Einfamilienhaus	*detached house; single-family home*
die Miete	*rent*
das Eßzimmer	dining room
das Wohnzimmer	living room
die Küche	kitchen
das WC	WC; toilet
das Erdgeschoß	ground floor
das Hochhaus	block of flats; apartment building
das Reihenhaus	terraced house
die Wohnung	flat; apartment
der Stock (4. Stock)	floor (4th floor)

Seite 32   Page 32

der, die, das	the → see contrastive notes, p. 31
die Familie	family
Das ist Familie Komischmann.	This is the Komischmann family.
	→ see contrastive notes, p. 31
das Kind, die Kinder (Pl.)	child, children
Herr und Frau Komischmann	Mr. and Mrs. Komischmann
und 3 Kinder.	and three children.
haben	to have
Sie haben eine Wohnung in Seltsam.	They have a flat in Seltsam.
die Toilette	toilet
groß	large
Die Wohnung ist groß.	The flat is large.
hell	light; bright
Das Schlafzimmer ist groß und hell.	The bedroom is large and bright.
sehr	very
Das Badezimmer ist auch sehr groß.	The bathroom is also very large.
klein	small

24

dunkel	dark
Das Wohnzimmer ist klein und dunkel.	The living room ist small and dark.
der Flur, -e	hall
ein, eine, ein	a → see contrastive notes, p. 31
ein Flur, eine Wohnung, ein Bad	a hall, a flat, a living room
die Couch, -es (11)	couch; sofa
der Tisch, -e (2)	table
der Stuhl, ¨e (4)	chair
das Bett, -en (10)	bed
der Schrank, -¨e (7)	cupboard
der Sessel, - (3)	easy chair; armchair
der Teppich, -e (12)	carpet; rug
die Lampe, -n (8)	lamp

Seite 33	**Page 33**

die Badewanne, -n (1)	bathtub
die Dusche, -n (6)	shower
das Waschbecken, - (9)	wash-basin; sink
das WC, -s (5)	lavatory, toilet
meinen	to think
Was meinen Sie?	What do you think?
besser	better
Wie ist es besser	How could it be better?
kein	no, not a → see contrastive notes, p. 31
sondern	but; but rather → see contrastive notes, p. 31
Zimmer A ist kein Schlafzimmer, sondern besser eine Küche.	Room A is not a bedroom, but more like a kitchen.
Nr. (= Nummer)	no. (number)
Nr. 4, wie heißt das auf deutsch?	No. 4, what is that in German?
doch	→ see contrastive notes, p. 31
Das ist doch kein Bett. – Doch!	That can't possibly be a bed. – But sure, it is!

Seite 34	**Page 34**

das Dorf, ¨er	village
die Fabrik, -en	factory
die Wassermühle, -n	water mill
der Platz, ¨e	square
das Bauernhaus, ¨er	farmhouse

die Kirche, -n	church
die Mühle, -n	mill
die Stadt, ⸚e	town
das Wohnhaus, ⸚er	private house; residential house
Süddeutschland	Southern Germany
eine Stadt in Süddeutschland.	a town in Southern Germany
das Jahr, -e	year
Die Stadt ist 800 Jahre alt.	The town is 800 years old.
der Einwohner, -	inhabitant
Die Stadt hat 11 800 Einwohner.	The town has 11 800 inhabitants.
die Leute	people
Hier arbeiten 8 000 Leute.	8 000 people work here.
produzieren	to produce
das Auto, -s	car
Die Fabrik produziert Autos.	The factory produces cars.
im (→ in dem)	in the
Ein Dorf im Engadin.	A village in the Engadin region.
Norddeutschland	Northern Germany
Das ist eine Wassermühle in Norddeutschland.	This is a water mill in Northern Germany.
jetzt	now
Die Mühle ist jetzt ein Wohnhaus.	The mill is now a home.
es gibt (→ geben)	there is
Es gibt ein Zimmer.	There is one room.

Seite 35   Page 35

finden	to find
der Stuhl, ⸚e	chair
Wie finden Sie die Stühle?	What do you think of the chairs?
praktisch	practical
Der Stuhl iat praktisch.	The chair is practical.
schön	attractive
häßlich	ugly
unpraktisch	impractical
alt	old
modern	modern
unmodern	old-fashioned
bequem	comfortable
unbequem	uncomfortable
die Lampe, -n	lamp
Und wie finden Sie die Lampen?	And what do you think of the lamps?

26

der, die, das	→ see contrastive notes, p. 31
du	→ see contrastive notes, p. 32
phantastisch	fantastic
Du, das Wohnzimmer ist phantastisch.	Don't you think this living room is fantastic?
gemütlich	cosy
Ja, das Wohnzimmer ist gemütlich.	Yes, the living room is very cosy.
die Möbel	furniture → see contrastive notes, p. 32
... und die Möbel sind sehr schön.	... and the furniture is very nice.
alle	all
Nicht alle, nur der Schrank.	Not all of them, only the cupboard.
toll	smashing; great
Und die Lampe, die ist toll.	And the lamp is smashing.
Die gefällt mir. (→ gefallen)	I like it. → see contrastive notes, p. 32
prima	first class
Das Wohnzimmer ist prima.	The living room is first class.
schlecht	bad
Das Wohnzimmer ist nicht schlecht.	The living room is not bad.

zu vermieten	to let
das Haus, ⁻er	house
der Bungalow, -s	*bungalow*
die Wohnfläche, -n	*living space, area*
die Zweizimmerwohnung, -en	*two-room flat*
die Nebenkosten	*extras*
die Kaution, -en	*deposit*
teuer	expensive
Wie teuer?	How expensive?
DM (= Deutsche Mark)	DM (= German Mark)
beschreiben	to describe
Beschreiben Sie:	Describe:
Die Wohnung liegt in Frankfurt.	→ see contrastive notes, p. 32
kosten	to cost
die Mark (= DM)	mark (= DM)
Sie kostet 430.– Mark.	It costs 430 mark.
es	it
Es (das Haus) ist groß.	It (the house) is large.

das Wohnen

Wohnen in der Bundesrepublik
Deutschland.

Preisspiegel für Wohnungsmieten

die Großstadt, ̈e

billig

Wo ist Wohnen billig?

die Altbauwohnung, -en

die Neubauwohnung, -en

living

Living in the Federal Republic of
Germany.

price guide to rents

city

cheap

Where is it cheap to live?

pre-war flat; old apartment

post-war flat; new apartment

ruhige Lage

Tel. (= Telefon)

16 Uhr

die Zeitung, -en

Die Wohnung in der Zeitung, ist die
noch frei?

Aha!

Aha. Und was kostet sie?

sofort

Ich möchte sofort kommen.

Geht das? (→ gehen)

er, sie, es

Nein, sie ist leider schon weg.

leider

weg

Oh, schade.

Vielen Dank.

der Quadratmeter, -

62 Quadratmeter.

die Straße, -n

die Adresse, -n

Wie ist die Adresse?

quiet place

telephone number

4 o'clock p. m.

newspaper

The flat (advertised) in the paper, is
it still vacant?

Ah!

Ah! And what does it cost?

at once; straightaway

I would like to come at once.

Is that all right?

it → see contrastive notes, p. 32

No, I'm afraid it's already taken.

unfortunately; I'm afraid

gone

Oh, what a pity!; Oh, that's too bad.

Many thanks.

square metre

62 square metres.

street, road

address

What is the address?

wir

suchen

Wir suchen ein neues Haus.

eins

we

to look for → see contrastive notes, p. 32

We are looking for a new house.

one

Wir haben eins in Bruchköbel.	*We have one in Bruchköbel.*
verdienen	*to earn*
im Monat	*a month, per month*
Ich verdiene nur 2 900,– Mark im Monat.	*I earn only 2 900 marks a month.*
der Kilometer, -	*kilometre*
die Verkehrsverbindung, -en	*communications (in public transport)*
Das ist 20 Kilometer von Bruchköbel.	*That is 20 km from Bruchköbel.*
der Bus, -se	*bus*
die Bahn, -en	*railway; railroad*
wenig	*few*
das Geschäft, -e	*shop; store*
Und dann gibt es hier nur wenige Geschäfte.	*And then there are only few shops here.*
die Person, -en	*person*
5 Personen.	*5 persons.*
pro	*per*
pro Monat.	*per month.*
die Hausfrau, -en	*housewife*
Frau Werner ist Hausfrau.	*Mrs. Werner is a housewife.*
positiv	*positive*
Was ist für Herrn Werner positiv/negativ?	*What is positive/negative for Herr Werner?*
negativ	*negative*
für	*for*
zwar	*of course*
Hier ist zwar alles nicht weit.	*Of course, everything is nearby here.*
alles	*everything*
weit	*far*
die Schule, -n	*school*
das Kino, -s	*cinema*
. . . und so weiter	*etcetera, etc.*
laut	*noisy*
Die Wohnung ist leider sehr laut.	*Unfortunately, the flat is very noisy.*
direkt	*right, exactly*
Sie liegt direkt im Stadtzentrum.	*It is right in the town centre.*
das Stadtzentrum, -tren	*town centre*
beide	both
Herr und Frau Krause arbeiten beide.	Herr and Frau Krause both work.
suchen	to look for
Suchen Sie eine neue Wohnung?	Are you looking for a new flat?
lesen	to read

Lesen Sie die Anzeigen auf Seite 37. Read the adverts on page 37.
die Anzeige, -n   advert

Seite 41   ## Page 41

die Wohnungssuche   looking for a flat/an apartment
der Text   text
  Ergänzen Sie den Text.   Complete the text.
mieten   to rent
  Herr Andoljsek möchte ... mieten   Mr Andoljsek would like to rent ...
bekommen   to get
  Er bekommt das Zimmer nicht.   But he doesn't get the room.
ruhig   quiet
  Das Haus liegt ruhig.   The house is in a quiet location.
schön   nice
  Das Zimmer ist schön groß.   The room is nice and large.
die Frage, -n   question
  Beantworten Sie dann die Fragen.   Then answer the questions.

Seite 42   ## Page 42

alternativ   *alternative*
  Wohnen – alternativ   *Alternative living*
Herr P. zeigt seinen Gästen die neue *Mr. P. shows his guests the new flat/*
  Wohnung.   *apartment.*
schlafen   *to sleep*
  Da schlafen wir.   *That's where we sleep.*
wir   *we*
  Da schlafen wir.   *That's where we sleep.*
Wie interessant!   *How interesting!*
immer   *always*
  Ja, wir schlafen immer in der Küche.   *Yes, we always sleep in the kitchen.*
kochen   *to cook*
  Und wo kochen Sie?   *And where do you cook?*
wirklich   *really*
  Sie kochen wirklich im Schlaf-   *You really cook in the bedroom?*
  zimmer?
wohl   *presumably*
  Das ist wohl das Bad?   *That's presumably the bathroom?*
originell   *original*
  Aber es ist sehr originell.   *But it is very original.*
baden   *to bathe, to take a bath*

Und hier das Wohnzimmer, da baden wir	*And here is the living room, this is where we take a bath.*
leben	*to live*
Wir leben nun mal alternativ.	*We go in for "alternative living".*
das stimmt.	*That's right!*
essen	*to eat*
Wir möchten jetzt essen.	*Now we want to eat.*
mit	→
Sie essen doch mit?	*Won't you eat with us?*
O Gott!	*Oh dear!*
die Zeit	*time*
Ich habe leider keine Zeit.	*I'm afraid I haven't got time.*

Contrastive notes

der, die, das (page 32): These words all mean *the*. Since there are no obvious indicators as to which one is correct for a given noun, you will have to memorize not just nouns, but always nouns together with their definite article. The article tells the gender of a noun, *der* being masculine, *die* feminine and *das* neuter. Note that in the plural, all nouns take *die* as their article.

Das ist Familie Komischmann. (page 32): In this sentence, *das* is not an article but a demonstrative pronoun corresponding to English *this* or *that*.

ein, eine (pages 32 and 128): *Ein* and *eine* are indefinite articles. As is shown in the table on page 128, *ein* is used for masculine and neuter nouns, *eine* for feminine nouns. In the plural, no article is used for indefinite nouns.

kein, keine (pages 33 and 128): *Kein* and *keine* are indefinite negative articles and mean *not a, not any, no. Kein* is used for masculine and neuter nouns, *keine* for feminine nouns and all plurals.

sondern (page 33): *Sondern* is used, as it were, to underscore the correction of a false statement: *Das ist kein Schlafzimmer, sondern ein Bad. – This is not a bedroom, but a bathroom.*

doch (page 33): *Das ist doch kein Bett. – Doch!* The first speaker uses *doch* to express bewilderment and disbelief ("That cannot possibly be a bed!"), whereas the second speaker uses *doch* to contradict a negative statement *(That cannot possibly be a bed. – But sure, it is.)*; in the same way, *doch* is used to contradict negative questions.

der, die, das (pages 36 and 128): In spoken German, the definite articles are used as definite pronouns, too. They substitute for a noun that was mentioned before, e. g.

Die Möbel sind sehr schön. Sind die neu?

Der Tisch ist schön. Ist der neu?

Du, ... (page 36): *Du* can serve as a "statement opener" roughly corresponding to *Hey, listen, ...*

die Möbel (page 36): *Die Möbel* is plural in German, though singular in English. German says e. g. *Die Möbel sind neu.*

Die gefällt mir. (page 36): While in English we say *I like it*, German turns the sentence around to an equivalent of *It appeals to me.*

Die Wohnung liegt in Frankfurt. Das Haus liegt schön. (page 37): In both these sentences, something is said about the location of the flat and the house, as is indicated by the verb, *liegen.* But note that while in the first sentence, *liegt* could be replaced by *ist* (as in English), this could not be done in the second sentence, because *schön* refers to the <u>location</u> of the house, not to the house itself.

suchen (page 40): *Suchen* means *to look for*; note that in German you do not need a preposition (for instance, *für*) to go with this verb: *Ich suche eine Wohnung.*

ihr (page 129): *Ihr* is the plural equivalent of *du.*

er, sie, es (page 39): *Er, sie* and *es* are personal pronouns. They substitute for a previously mentioned noun and mean *she, he* or *it. Er* takes the place of masculine nouns in the singular, *sie* of feminine and *es* of neuter nouns only. For all plural nouns, *sie* is used.

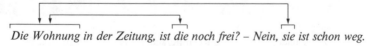

Die Wohnung in der Zeitung, ist die noch frei? – Nein, sie ist schon weg.

Sie is used for female persons even if the grammatical gender of the noun is neuter, as is the case with *das Fräulein.*

Seite 43	Page 43
essen	to eat
trinken	to drink
das Obst	fruit
der Käse	cheese
die Wurst, ⸚e	sausage
die Kartoffel, -n	potato
der Salat, -e	lettuce
der Reis	rice
die Milch	milk
das Gemüse	vegetables
der Fisch, -e	fish
das Wasser	water
der Wein	wine
die Butter	butter
das Fleisch	meat
das Ei, -er	egg
das Glas, ⸚er	glass
das Bier, -e	beer
das Brot, -e	bread
die Gabel, -n	fork
der Löffel, -	spoon
der Teller, -	plate
der Kuchen, -	cake
das Messer, -	knife
das Ei, -er	egg

Seite 44/45	Page 44/45
der Rentner, die Rentnerin	pensioner (m; f)
das Frühstück	breakfast
das Mittagessen, -	lunch
der Kaffee (= die Kaffeezeit)	mid-afternoon coffee time
das Abendessen, -	supper
zu Hause	at home
in der Kantine (die Kantine)	in the canteen
im Büro (das Büro)	in (at) the office
im Café (das Café)	in the cafe

in der Universität (die Universität)	in the university
im Schnellimbiß (der Schnellimbiß)	in the snack bar
das Brötchen, -	roll; bun
1 Brötchen mit Marmelade.	1 roll and jam
mit	with
die Marmelade	jam
der Kaffee	coffee
Er trinkt Kaffee.	He drinks coffee.
das Butterbrot, -e	sandwich
2 Butterbrote mit Käse	2 cheese sandwiches
nichts	nothing
das Käsebrot, -e	open sandwich with cheese
die Rindfleischsuppe, -n	beef soup
die Suppe, -n	soup
der Tee	tea
das Kotelett, -s	chop
der Salat	salad
die Flasche, -n	bottle → see contrastive notes, p. 41
1 Flasche Bier	1 bottle of beer
das Wurstbrot, -e	open sandwich with cold sliced sausage
das Mineralwasser, -	mineral water
Was ißt Herr Meinen? (→ essen)	What does Mr Meinen eat?
ein, einen	a → see contrastive notes, p. 40
zum Frühstück	→
Zum Frühstück ißt Herr Meinen ein Brötchen.	For breakfast Mr Meinen eats a roll.
später	later
Später trinkt Herr Meinen einen Kaffee.	Later Mr Meinen drinks a cup of coffee.
gerne	→ see contrastive notes, p. 41
Essen Sie gerne Kotelett?	Do you like eating chops?
gern	→ see contrastive notes, p. 41
Ja, sehr gern.	Yes, very much.
zu	too
Nein, das ist zu fett.	No, that's got too much fat.
fett	fat, rich
lieber	→ see contrastive notes, p. 41
Ich esse lieber Hähnchen.	I prefer eating chicken.
das Hähnchen, -	chicken
die Gulaschsuppe, -n	goulash soup
sauer	sour
süß	sweet

scharf	hot, highly spiced, spicy
bitter	bitter
viel	a lot
man	→ see contrastive notes, p. 41
Ißt man bei Ihnen viel Kartoffeln?	Does they eat potatoes a lot where you come from?
die Trinkmilch	*milk*
die Südfrucht, ¨e	*tropical fruit*
der Zucker	*sugar*
das Fett, -e	*fat*
vor 30 Jahren	*30 years ago*
heute	*today*

Seite 46 — Page 46

kalte Vorspeisen	*cold starters*
warme Vorspeisen	*warm starters*
das Hauptgericht, -e	*main dish*
vom Schwein	*pork*
vom Rind	*beef*
das Dessert, -s	*dessert*
das Getränk, -e	drink; beverage
welche? (Pl.)	which?
Welche Wörter kennen Sie?	Which words do you know?
kennen	to know
das Gericht, -e	dish
das Land, ¨er	country
Was gibt es auch in Ihrem Land?	What do you have in your country too?
der Kalbsrahmbraten, -	*roast veal in cream*
die Gemüsesuppe	→ see contrastive notes, p. 42
das Rindersteak, -s	*beef steak*
der Nachtisch	dessert
das Vanilleeis	vanilla ice cream
zuordnen	to arrange
Ordnen Sie zu:	Sort out the following:
das Schweinefleisch	pork
das Rindfleisch	beef
das Kalbfleisch	veal
das Schweinefilet	*filet of pork*

35

Seite 47	Page 47
der Orangensaft, ⸚e	orange juice
dick	fat
Jetzt sind Sie zu dick.	Now you are too fat.
sagen	to say, to tell
die Tasse, -n	cup

Seite 48	Page 48
bestellen	to order
Wir möchten gern bestellen.	We would like to order.
bitte	please
Bitte, was bekommen Sie?	What would you like?
nehmen	to take, to have → see contrastive notes, p. 41
Ich nehme eine Gemüsesuppe und einen Salatteller.	I'll have a vegetable soup and a salad.
der Salatteller, -	salad
der Weißwein	white wine
ein Glas Weißwein	a glass of white wine
das Steak	steak
Ein Steak bitte.	A steak, please.
die Pommes frites	chips, french fries
Aber keine Pommes frites.	But without chips.
der Apfelsaft, ⸚e	apple juice
bitte schön (→ bitte)	→ see contrastive notes, p. 41
der Rotwein	red wine
leider nicht	→
Nein, leider nicht.	No, I'm afraid not.

Seite 49	Page 49
bezahlen	to pay
Wir möchten bezahlen.	We would like to pay.
zusammen	→
Zusammen oder getrennt?	One bill or separate bills?
getrennt	separately
die Forelle, -n	trout
Das macht 19.50 DM.	That comes to 19.50 DM.
der Wein	wine
das Schinkenbrot, -e	open sandwich with ham
der Ober, -	waiter

entschuldigen	→
Oh, entschuldigen Sie.	Oh, I'm sorry.
kalt	cold
der Schweinebraten, -	roast pork
frisch	fresh
die Roulade, -n	beef olive (slice of beef rolled and stuffed)

Seite 50 — Page 50

Preisinformation, -en	price list
die Schlagsahne	*whipped cream*
1 (= Liter)	1 (= litre)
der Joghurt	*yoghurt*
der Becher, -	mug, carton
die Margarine	*margarine*
g (= Gramm)	g (gramme)
die Vollmilch	*unskimmed milk*
die Packung, -en	packet, package
das Öl, -e	oil
das Papiertaschentuch, -er	*tissue*
der Sekt	*German champagne*
das Pils	*lager*
die Dose, -n	can
das Vollwaschmittel, -	*detergent for all fabrics*
Kg (= Kilogramm)	kg (kilogramme)
die Nudel, -n	*noodle*
das Paket, -e	*packet, package*
der Zucker	*sugar*
das Weizenmehl, -e	*flour*
geschälte ganze Tomaten	*whole peeled tomatoes*
der Champignon	*mushroom*
der Thunfisch	*tuna fish*
brauchen	to need
Was brauchen wir noch?	What else do we need?
noch	→ see contrastive notes, p. 41
kaufen	to buy
Was haben die beiden gekauft?	What did the two of them buy?

Seite 51 — Page 51

schmecken	to taste
Schmeckt der Fisch?	Does the fish taste all right?

etwas → see contrastive notes, p. 41/42

  Nehmen Sie doch noch etwas!   Do have some more!

genug enough

  Nein danke, ich habe noch genug.   Thank you, I still have enough.

satt →

  Danke, ich bin satt.   Thank you, I have had enough.

mehr more

  Danke, ich möchte nicht mehr.   Thank you, I don't want any more.

die Krötensuppe *toad soup*

  Ich esse lieber Krötensuppe.   *I prefer toad soup.*

die Zwiebel, -n onion

der Schinken ham

die Gurke cucumber

das Mehl flour

Seite 52   Page 52

Einladung zum Essen invitation to a meal

Beurteilen Sie die folgenden Sätze: Decide whether the following sentences

richtig (r) / falsch (f) / ich weiß nicht (?). are: true (t) / false (f) / don't know (?).

folgend following

der Satz, ¨e sentence

der Freund, -e friend

  Die 3 Freunde essen keine Vorspeise.   The 3 friends are having no starter.

als as

  Sie essen Salat als Vorspeise   They are having salad as a starter.

zum (als) Nachtisch as a dessert

Seite 53   Page 53

Probieren geht über studieren. *The proof of the pudding is in the eating.*
(lit.: to try it out is better than to think
about it)

ca. (= circa) *about, approximately*

das Kilo (= Kilogramm) kilo

das Salz *salt*

der Pfeffer *pepper*

der Curry *curry powder*

der Thymian *thyme*

das Basilikum *basil*

die Fleischbrühe, -n *stock*

das Pfund, -e *pound, half kilo*

rot *red*

rote Zwiebeln	*French onions*
die Mandel, -n	*almond*
die Petersilie	*parsley*
kochen	to cook
das Stück, -e	piece
Die Hähnchen in Stücke schneiden.	Cut the chicken into pieces.
schneiden	*to cut*
würzen	*to spice*
braten	*to fry*
dazugeben (→ geben)	*to add*
Die Fleischbrühe dazugeben.	*Add the stock.*
schälen	*to peel*
nochmal	→
nochmal 10 Minuten kochen.	*Cook for another 10 minutes.*
bestreuen	*to garnish*
Das Essen mit Petersilie bestreuen.	*Garnish with parsley.*
servieren	*to serve*
Reis und Hähnchen servieren.	*Serve the rice and chicken.*

Seite 54   Page 54

ein schwieriger Gast	*a difficult customer*
dann	*then*
Dann bitte ein Glas Käse!	*Then a glass of cheese, please!*
meinen	*to mean*
Sie meinen: ein Stück Käse?	*You mean: a piece of cheese?*
der Kartoffelsalat	*potato salad*
tut mir leid (→ tun)	*I'm sorry*
was (= etwas)	*something*
die Limonade	*lemonade*
Verzeihung	→
Verzeihung, einen Teller Bier haben wir nicht.	*Forgive me, we do not have a plate of beer.*
überhaupt	→
Was haben Sie denn überhaupt?	*Well what have you got, then?*
zum Beispiel	*for example*
Nun, wir haben zum Beispiel . . .	*Well, for instance, we have . . .*
das Omelett, -s	*omelet*

Contrastive notes

einen, den (pages 44 and 130): Look for the following sentences in the table on page 130:

Das ist   ein   Kuchen.
Sie ißt   einen Kuchen.
Sie nimmt einen Kuchen.

In each case, *Kuchen* shows up in the position of "obligatorische Ergänzung" ("compulsory supplement"). Yet there is a difference: The article in the first sentence is *ein,* in the second and third sentences, it is *einen*. Obviously, in these two cases, *Kuchen* is a different kind of "obligatorische Ergänzung". But why?

The first sentence is like an equation, the verb *ist* serving as an "equals sign" between demonstrative pronoun and the noun. Not so in the other sentences: Here, something is done by somebody with something. These sentences are not, as it were, in equilibrium, and it may therefore be important to make clear, by some grammatical means, which part of a sentence denotes the "doer" of the action indicated by the verb and which part denotes the thing (or person) at which (whom) this action is directed. (In English, the word order is basically sufficient to make this distinction, but in German the word order can be varied quite a bit.)

The "compulsory supplement" denoting the person or thing at whom/which an action is being directed – in our examples, *der Kuchen* – is called " Akkusativergänzung" ("accusative supplement"). Masculine nouns take on the articles *einen, keinen* or *den* when standing in a sentence as "Akkusativergänzung" to a verb like *nehmen* or *essen*; however, feminine and neuter nouns do not change the form of their articles when they function as "Akkusativergänzung".

On page 130 you will find, under *b*), *Artikelformen im Akkusativ*, the articles for the accusative; and under *c*), *Verben mit Akkusativergänzung*, further verbs with "Akkusativergänzung" are listed. Note that the phrase *es gibt* has to be used with accusative, too!

Inversion (page 131): We are familiar with interrogatives (like *Was . . . ?*) causing "inversion", which means that the subject shows up in the position after the verb (see page 15). Likewise, other parts of a sentence can come to the front position and cause inversion.

This can be an "*Angabe*" (from the position tinted green); by moving such an "additional information" into first position, its emphasis can be slightly increased and the sentence connected more closely to the previous one. *Zum Frühstück ißt er ein Brötchen.:* The emphasis is on both *breakfast* (as opposed to any other meal) and *a roll* (as opposed to any other food one might eat for breakfast.)

On the other hand, an "obligatorische Ergänzung" (from the position tinted light blue) can equally move into the first position of the sentence and cause inversion. Usually, this is

40

done to stress some contrast (as in English). *Suppe esse ich nicht; Salat esse ich gerne.:* The emphasis is on the *soup*, which I don't like, and on the *salad*, which I like.

Note that *Ja* and *Nein* do not cause inversion.

Plurals (page 129): There is no single way of forming the plural in German. Although it is possible to distinguish certain groups of plural forms, it is much more economic for you to simply learn the plural for each noun, just as you learn its article, too.

eine Flasche Bier (page 44): In contrast to English *a bottle of beer,* note the absence of a preposition in the German phrase.

gern, gerne, lieber (page 45): *Gern* and *gerne* are interchangeable and mean that you like doing something. Simply add them after the appropriate verb, e. g. *Ich trinke gern Wein.* A preference can be expressed by adding *lieber*, e. g. *Ich trinke lieber Bier.*

man (page 45): The use of *man* corresponds to the use in English of *people, one* or the non-specific *they* in a question like *Do they eat potatoes a lot where you come from? – Ißt man bei Ihnen viel Kartoffeln?*

bitte schön (page 48): This phrase is often used to ask what someone wants to get, wants to order or wants to know. The corresponding phrase in English would be *Yes, please?* or *Can I help you?*
A second use of *bitte schön* is as a response to *Danke.*, similar to the English *You are welcome.*

Nehmen Sie! Nimm! (pages 51 and 131): These are orders or commands. Use the form *Nehmen Sie . . . !* when speaking to people you address as *Sie* and the form *Nimm . . . !* for people you address as *du.* On page 131 you will find rules for the forming of the imperative. But be careful: Used without modifiers, an imperative can sound quite rude and produce an effect very different from what you may have intended.
Suggestions often come in the shape of an imperative softened by the modifier *doch*; the same combination of imperative and *doch* can also be used to urge hospitality on one's guests:
Bezahl die Milch doch morgen!
Nehmen Sie doch noch Suppe!

nehmen (page 48): When ordering food or drinks in a restaurant, the correct verb to use is *nehmen. Haben* is wrong in this context and would probably not be immediately understood.

noch (pages 50 and 51): *Noch* is a modifier which you can use when you want to add something to what you already have, e. g. *Nehmen Sie doch noch etwas Fisch!* On the other hand, *noch* is also used to indicate that there is still something left, e. g. *Nein danke, ich habe noch genug.*

Gemüsesuppe (page 46): In German, new nouns can be formed by combining two nouns. The second of these two nouns conveys the basic meaning of this new compound noun and defines its gender; the first noun of the two narrows down or specifies the meaning of the second. E. g., *Gemüsesuppe* is soup – therefore feminine *(die Suppe)* – , but more specifically, it is soup made from vegetables and not just any kind of soup.

In most cases, English tends to simply put the two nouns next to each other, e. g. *vegetable soup*; in some cases, the two nouns will be hyphenated.

Lektion 5   Kursbuch

Seite 55	Page 55
Montag	Monday
Dienstag	Tuesday
Mittwoch	Wednesday
Donnerstag	Thursday
Freitag	Friday
Samstag	Saturday
Sonntag	Sunday
leben	to live, to exist, to be alive
Arbeiten ist leben.	To work is to live.
schreiben	to write
putzen	to clean, to sweep
der Fußball, ⁻e	football
Fußball spielen.	to play football
spielen	to play
fotografieren	to photograph
fernsehen	to watch television
lesen	to read
treffen	to meet
Freunde treffen	to meet friends
die Musik	music
Musik machen	to make music

42

Seite 56	Page 56

Willkommen an Bord.   *Welcome on board.*

Seite 57	Page 57

das Deck, -s	deck
das Schwimmbad, ¨er	swimming pool
die Bar, -s	bar
das Restaurant, -s	restaurant
das Sportzentrum, -tren	sports centre
das Fitneßzentrum, -tren	fitness centre
die Kabine, -n	cabin
die Bibliothek, -en	library
der Friseur, -e	hairdresser (m.)
das Geschäft, -e	shop
die Bank, -en	bank
die Metzgerei, -en	butcher's
das Krankenhaus, ¨er	hospital
das Kino, -s	cinema
die Maschine, -n	engine
auf	on
auf Deck	on deck
flirten	to flirt
spazieren gehen	to go for a walk
schwimmen	to swim
Wo schwimmt jemand?	Where is someone swimming?
jemand	someone
schlafen	to sleep
kochen	to cook
tanzen	to dance
einkaufen	to shop → see contrastive notes, p. 48
das Tischtennis	table tennis
Wo spielt jemand Tischtennis?	Where is someone playing table tennis?

Seite 58	Page 58

fünf Uhr	five o'clock
halb zehn	half past nine, nine thirty
	→ see contrastive notes, p. 49
der Kellner, die Kellnerin	waiter
der Koch, ¨e	cook (m.)
der Architekt, die Architektin	architect

aufstehen	to get up → see contrastive notes, p. 48
anfangen	to begin → see contrastive notes, p. 48
Frank fängt seine Arbeit an.	Frank starts work.
die Arbeit	work
Betten machen	to make beds
macht Betten.	makes (the) beds
holen	to fetch, to get
holt Fisch	fetches fish
bringen	to bring
bringt Medikamente	brings medicines
das Medikament, -e	medicine
schneiden	to cut
Klaus schneidet Kartoffeln.	Klaus cuts potatoes.
frühstücken	to have breakfast
aufräumen	to tidy up → see contrastive notes, p. 48
das Buch, ¨-er	book
liest ein Buch.	reads a book
wann?	when?
Wann steht Frank Michel auf?	When does Frank Michel get up?
beschreiben	to describe
Beschreiben Sie:	Describe (the pictures):
um	at
Er steht um fünf Uhr auf.	He gets up at five o'clock.

Seite 59   Page 59

aufschreiben	to write down
die Bestellung, -en	order
Er schreibt die Bestellung auf.	He takes the order.
schlafen gehen	to go to sleep
Er geht schlafen.	He goes to sleep.
die Pause, -n	break
Anne macht Pause.	Anne is taking a break.
der Verband, ¨-e	the bandage
Sie macht einen Verband.	She puts on a bandage.
ausgeben	to dish up
Klaus gibt Essen aus.	Klaus dishes up the food.
noch	→ see contrastive notes, p. 49
Er trinkt noch ein Bier.	He has another beer.
zu Mittag essen	to have lunch
Sie ißt zu Mittag.	She is having lunch.

kann (→ können)
 Was kann man hier machen?
die Discothek, -en
geöffnet (→ öffnen)
 Wann geöffnet?
der Weinkeller, -
wohin?
 Wohin denn?
nachher
 Gehen wir nachher noch weg?
noch
weggehen
mitgehen
 Gehen Sie nachher noch mit?
ins (= in das)
 Ins Café Lug.

can
 What can one do here?
discotheque
open
 When is it open?
wine cellar
Where to?
 Where shall we go?
Afterwards
 Shall we go out afterwards?
→ see contrastive notes, p. 49
to go out
to come along
 Will you come along too afterwards?
→ see contrastive notes, p. 49
 To the Lug Cafe.

wieder
 Ich möchte mal wieder essen gehen.
mitkommen
 Kommst du mit?
vielleicht
kannst (→ können)
 Kannst du Montag abend?
Montag abend

Um vieviel Uhr?
So um acht.
Tut mir leid.
da
muß (→ müssen)
 Ich muß arbeiten.
die Woche, -n
nächste Woche
 Ich möchte nächste Woche
 essen gehen.
essen gehen

again
 I'd like to go out for a meal again.
to come along
 Are you coming along, too?
perhaps
(you) can
 Can you manage Monday evening?
Monday evening → see contrastive
 notes, p. 49
At what time?
About eight.
I'm sorry.
→ see contrastive notes, p. 49
must → see contrastive notes, p. 49
 I must work.
week
next week
 I'd like to go out for a meal
 next week.
to go aut for a meal → see contrastive
 notes, p. 49

das Theater	theatre
das Konzert, -e	concert
Hast du Lust?	Do you feel like (coming)?
Zeit haben	to have time
Hast du Zeit?	Have you got time?
der Deutschkurs, -e	German course

Seite 62   Page 62

alles	→
Was muß Frau Herbst alles machen?	What does Frau Herbst have to do?
der Buchhändler, -in	bookseller (m; f)
pro	per
Sie arbeitet 40 Std. pro Woche.	She works 40 hours per week.
rodeln	*to go toboganning*
laufen	*to walk, to run*
Skilanglauf machen	*to go cross-country skiing*
radfahren	*to ride a bicycle*
Schach spielen	*to play chess*
Ball spielen	*to play ball*
parken	*to park*
grillen	*to have a barbecue*
die Gaststätte	*restaurant*
der Radweg	*cycle track*
die Bademöglichkeit	*swimming permitted, a place to swim*

Seite 63   Page 63

das Viertel	quarter
Es ist erst Viertel nach acht.	It is only a quarter past eight.
nach	past
heute	today
Was macht Birgit heute abend?	What is Birgit doing this evening?
noch einmal	once more, once again
Hören Sie den Dialog noch einmal.	Listen to the dialogue once more.
ansehen	to look at
Sehen Sie den Terminkalender an.	Look at the diary.
der Terminkalender, -	diary
vergleichen	to compare
Vergleichen Sie:	Compare:

Das Institut für Arbeitsmarkt- *und Berufsforschung*	*Institute for employment* *and job research*
fragen	to ask
die Antwort, -en	*answer*
verschieden	*different*
verschiedene Länder	*different countries*
das Prozent, -e	*per cent*
stolz sein auf	*to be proud of*
Sind Sie stolz auf Ihre Arbeit?	*Are you proud of your work?*
antworten	*to answer*
Was antworten Sie?	*What is your answer?*
überhaupt nicht	*not at all*
die Meinung, -en	*opinion*
Vergleichen Sie die Meinung . . .	*Compare the opinion . . .*
vergleichen mit	*to compare . . . . . with*

faul	*lazy*
Sind die Deutschen faul?	*Are the Germans lazy?*
bis	*up to*
fünfeinhalb bis sechs Tage	*five and a half to six days*
knapp	*barely*
knapp 5 Tage in der Woche	*barely 5 days a week*
höchstens	*at most; at the most*
Ein Japaner hat höchstens *20 Arbeitstage Urlaub.*	*A Japanese has at most* *20 working days holiday.*
der Urlaub, -e	*holiday, vacation*
ungefähr	*approximately*
im Schnitt	*on average; on the average*
In einem japanischen Betrieb sind *im Schnitt zwei bis drei Prozent* *der Mitarbeiter krank.*	*In a Japanese factory there are, on* *average, two to three per cent of the* *workforce off sick.*
das Prozent, -e	*per cent*
der Mitarbeiter, -	*colleague; fellow worker*
krank sein	*to be ill; sick*
ständig	*always*
In einem deutschen Betrieb sind *ständig zehn bis zwölf Prozent krank.*	*In a German factory there are always ten* *to twelve per cent sick.*
der Arbeitnehmer, -	*employee*
der Arbeitsmarkt, -̈e	*labour market*

der Mensch, -en	person
der Arbeitsplatz, ⁻e	job
bei gutem Wachstum	with good growth
bei mäßigem Wachstum	with moderate growth
jährlich	annually
die Situation, -en	situation
Wie ist die Situation in Ihrem Land?	What is the situation like in your country?

Seite 66	Page 66
der Feierabend, -e	finishing time; after work
die Idee, -n	idea
Hast du eine Idee?	Have you any ideas?
vorschlagen	to suggest
Ich schlage vor ...	I suggest ...
das Kabarett, -s	cabaret
offen gesagt	frankly
bleiben	to stay
Wir bleiben heute mal zu Hause.	Let's stay at home today.
wie immer	as always
wenigstens	at least
Das kostet wenigstens nichts.	At least that doesn't cost anything.
die Macher (→ machen)	doer
Wir Macher	We doers
der Sport	sports
die Politik	politics
der Fehler, -	mistake
die Dummheit, -en	blunder
der Quatsch	nonsense

Contrastive notes

jemand (page 57): German does not make the distinction between *somebody* and *anybody*, but uses *jemand* for either.

Wo kauft jemand ein? (pages 57, 58 and 132): Some German verbs consist of two elements, as in English *to get up* or *to tidy up*. But unlike English, the two parts of such German verbs stand apart from each other in different positions. On page 132, these two verb positions are tinted dark blue in table *2. Verben mit Verbzusatz*. The first verb position is occupied by the conjugated part of the verb (similar to the usage of *möchte*; cf. table 3 on page 127), the other part of the verb moves into the second verb position at the end of the sentence. However, in the infinitive – that is how you find them written in dictionaries – these verbs are written as one word, with the conjugated part in the rear.

einkaufen	*Wo kauft jemand ein?*
fernsehen	*Wo sieht jemand fern?*
aufstehen	*Wann steht Frank auf?*
anfangen	*Um sieben Uhr fängt er seine Arbeit an.*
aufräumen	*Um elf räumt er auf.*

Times (page 58): Rather than using an equivalent to the English *a. m.* or *p. m.*, Germans count 24 hours in a day and add the minutes, as in international time tables and flight tables.

When telling the time informally, the half hour does not refer back to the last full hour, as in English *half past nine*, but forward to the coming hour: *halb zehn*, meaning *half an hour left until ten o'clock*.

The half hour is used as a reference point for the "neighbouring" times, e. g. *9.25 Uhr* is *fünf Minuten vor halb zehn* or simply *fünf vor halb zehn*, and *9.35 Uhr* is *fünf nach halb zehn*.

wohin (page 60): German, unlike English, is consistent in making the distinction between *where* and *where to*, always using *wohin* when movement is concerned.

noch (pages 59 and 60): *Gehen wir nachher noch weg? Ich muß noch arbeiten.* In these sentences, *noch* is added to show that the action referred to is seen as an additional element in a schedule of activities which may be crowded already.

in den, in die, ins (page 60): German *in* followed by an accusative indicates movement into some place. People go *in die Diskothek, in den Weinkeller* or *ins Café* (*ins* is the contracted form of *in das*).

Montag abend (page 61): When finding variations on this dialogue, note that for *tonight*, German uses *heute abend*, and for *this morning*, *heute morgen*.

da (page 61): In colloquial German, *da* can serve as a pronoun, as it were, for a particular time which has just been mentioned, e. g.

Um acht? Tut mir leid, da kann ich nicht. Da muß ich arbeiten.

kannst du, ich muß (pages 61 and 132): *Kannst* and *muß* are conjugated forms of the modal verbs *können* and *müssen*. As in English, modal verbs are used together with the infinitive

49

of another verb. But remember that unlike English, that infinitive goes to the second verb position at the end of the sentence:

Ich kann Montag abend kommen.

Ich muß noch arbeiten.

Since it is the infinitive which is required, those verbs which split into two elements (like *aufräumen*) will stay in one piece when used together with a modal verb: *Ich muß die Wohnung aufräumen.*

Kannst du Montag abend? omits the infinitive verb because the question can be understood within the context.

Können has three meanings. The sentence *Sie können hier nicht Ski fahren.* can be understood to refer to the <u>ability</u> of doing something (*This slope is too steep for you!*); to the <u>possibility</u> of something being done (*Don't take your skis with you, there is no skiing here.*); or to <u>permission</u> being granted to do something (*Skiing is not permitted here!*). See Arbeitsbuch, page 50.

Sie gehen schwimmen. Sie gehen essen. (pages 62 and 132): In these sentences, the verb *gehen* uses the infinitive of another verb (*schwimmen*, *essen*) as a supplement. In English, the gerund of verbs is used in a similar way: *They go swimming.*

Lektion 6 Kursbuch

Seite 67	Page 67
von	by
der Schüler, -	pupil

Seite 68	Page 68
das Bild, -er	picture
zusammenpassen	to match; to go together
Was paßt zusammen?	Which go together?
das Schloß, ̈-er	*castle*
die Attraktion, -en	*attraction*
Das Schloß ist eine Attraktion für Touristen.	*The castle is a tourist attraction.*
für	*for*
der Tourist, -en	*tourist*
die Welt	*world*
aus aller Welt	*from all over the world*
das Ruhrgebiet	*Ruhr District*

das Industriezentrum, -en	industrial centre
dort	there
Dort leben 8,5 Millionen Menschen.	8.5 million people live there.
der Frühling	spring
der Sommer	summer
der Herbst	autumn
der Winter	winter
der Schwarzwald	Black Forest
immer	always
Der Schwarzwald ist immer schön.	The Black Forest is always beautiful.
besonders	especially
romantisch	romantic
Der Winter ist hier besonders romantisch	Winter is especially romantic here.
das Märchen, -	fairy tale
die Stadtmusikanten (Pl.)	city musicians
das Tier, -e	animal
nach	to → see contrastive notes, p. 57
wandern	to make one's way
Vier Tiere wandern nach Bremen.	4 animals make their way to Bremen.
darum	therefore
Darum sind sie jetzt das Symbol	That is why they are now the symbol
der Stadt Bremen.	of the city of Bremen.
der Rhein	the Rhine
fließen	to flow
durch	through
Er fließt durch die Schweiz.	It flows through Switzerland.
Holland	Holland
fahren	to go → see contrastive notes, p. 57
der Urlaub	holidays
in	→ see contrastive notes, p. 57
die Alpen (Pl.)	the Alps
Viele Deutsche fahren im Urlaub in	Many Germans go to the Alps for
die Alpen.	their holidays.
steigen	to climb
auf	to the top of → see contrastive notes, p. 57
Nicht alle steigen auf die Zugspitze.	Not everyone climbs the Zugspitze.
der höchste Berg (→ hoch)	the highest mountain
die Sonne	the sun
der Dom, -e	cathedral
typisch	typical
gotisch	Gothic
Eine typisch gotische Kirche.	A typical Gothic church.

die größte Kirche	*the largest church*
tausende	*thousands*
an	to → see contrastive notes, p. 57
die Ostsee	*the Baltic*
Tausende fahren an die Ostsee	*Thousands go to the Baltic,*
nach Travemünde.	*to Travemünde.*

Seite 69   Page 69

der Brocken	*Brocken mountain (where witches gather)*
die Postkarte	*postcard*
der Ortsname	*place name*
Ihr Lieben	*Dear friends*
das Wetter	*weather*
wahnsinnig	*dreadfully*
langweilig	*boring*
Es ist wahnsinnig langweilig.	*It is dreadfully boring.*
morgen	*tomorrow*
Morgen fahren wir ins Ruhrgebiet.	*Tomorrow we are going to the Ruhr District.*
liebe Grüße	*best wishes*

Seite 70   Page 70

das Luxus-Hotel, -s	*luxury hotel*
hervorragende Küche	*excellent cuisine*
besonders ruhig	*especially quiet*
das Zentrum, -en	*centre*
persönliche Atmosphäre	*a personal touch*
moderne Komforträume	*modern luxury rooms*
der Garten, ⸚	*garden*
fünf Minuten vom Zentrum	*five minutes from the centre*
der Balkon, -e	*balcony*
der Preis, -e	*price*
ruhige Lage	*quiet situation, quiet location*
welcher?, welche?, welches?	which? → see contrastive notes, p. 57
der Gasthof, ⸚e	inn
das Hotel, -s	hotel
die Pension, -en	guest house
ruhig	quiet
klimatisiert	→
Die Zimmer sind klimatisiert.	The rooms are air-conditioned.
das Privatzimmer, -	room with a family

52

Privatzimmer finde ich besser.	I prefer rooms with a family.
zentral	central
Aber die Pension Hubertushof	But the Pension Hubertushof is
liegt zentraler.	more central.
gut, besser, am besten	good, better, best → see contrastive notes, p. 57

Seite 71 / Page 71

suchen	to look for
Wir suchen ein Doppelzimmer für	We are looking for a room for
ungefähr 300 Schilling.	about 300 Schilling.
das Doppelzimmer, -	double room
ungefähr	about
der Schilling. -e	(Austrian) shilling
empfehlen	to recommend
Können Sie etwas empfehlen?	Can you recommend something?
ohne	without
Mit oder ohne Frühstück?	With or without breakfast?
weit	far
Wie weit ist es zum Zentrum?	How far is it to the centre?
das Zentrum, -en	centre
der Balkon, -e	balcony
Hat das Zimmer einen Balkon?	Does the room have a balcony?
das Einzelzimmer, -	single room
Ich suche ein Einzelzimmer.	I am looking for a single room.
möglichst	
möglichst zentral	as central as possible
direkt	right, directly
direkt im Zentrum	right in the centre
laut	noisy
Das ist zu laut.	That is too noisy.
5 Minuten zum (= zu dem) Zentrum	*5 minutes to the centre*

Seite 72 / Page 72

km (= der Kilometer)	km (kilometer)
dieses Jahr	this year
Wohin fahren Sie dieses Jahr?	Where are you going this year?
warm	warm
wenig	few
wenig Touristen	few tourists

das Verkehrsmittel, -	*means of transport*
die Autobahn, -en	*motorway; highway*
die Eisenbahn, -en	*railway*
der Flughafen, ⁻	*airport*
von	from
Wie weit ist es von Köln	How far is it from Cologne
nach München?	to Munich?
Wie kommt man von Münster	How can one get from Münster
nach Berlin?	to Berlin?
die Bahn, -en	railway, train
das Flugzeug, -e	aeroplane

der Preis, -e	*price*
2. Klasse	*2nd class*
umsteigen	*to change*
in Frankfurt umsteigen	*change in Frankfurt*
benutzen	to use
Benutzen Sie die Karte auf S. 73.	Use the map on p. 73.
die Karte, -n	map
dauern	to take time
Wie lange dauert der Flug?	How long does the flight take?
der Flug, ⁻e	flight
die Bahnfahrt, -en	train journey
die Autofahrt, -en	car journey
diskutieren	to discuss
Diskutieren Sie die Vorteile.	Discuss the advantages.
der Vorteil, -e	advantage
schnell	fast
kurz	short
der Nachteil, -e	disadvantage
kompliziert	complicated
anstrengend	tiring
der Stammtisch, -e	table in a restaurant or pub where a group of friends meet regularly
das Gespräch, -e	conversation
Hören Sie das Gespräch.	Listen to the conversation.
beantworten	to answer
Beantworten Sie die Fragen.	Answer the questions.

fliegen
  Ich möchte morgen nach Bremen fliegen.

to fly
  I would like to fly to Bremen tomorrow.

der Zug, ⸚e
  Welcher Zug ist am günstigsten?

train
  Which train is the best?

günstig

good; convenient

ankommen
  Der kommt um 13 Uhr an.

to arrive
  It arrives at 1 pm.

die Maschine, -n (= Flugzeug)
  Welche Maschine ist am günstigsten?

plane
  Which flight is the best?

der Bahnhof, ⸚e
  Auf dem Bahnhof.

station
  At the station.

der Intercity

Inter City train

abfahren
  Wo fährt der ab?

to leave
  Where does it leave?

das Gleis, -e

platform (literally: track)

die Verspätung, -en
  Aber der Zug hat Verspätung.

delay
  But the train is delayed.

die Ansage, -n

announcement

noch nicht
  Der D-242 ist noch nicht da.

not yet
  The D-242 has not yet arrived.

das Ferienzentrum, -en — *holiday centre*

zwischen — *between*

das Seeheilbad, ⸚er — *seaside health resort*

die Jahreszeit, -en — *season*

die Erholung, -en — *recreation*

das Spiel, -e — *games*

die Unterhaltung, -en — *entertainment*

die Turnhalle, -n — *gymnasium*

im Freien — *in the open air; outdoor*

täglich — *daily*

das Kinderparadies, -e — *paradise for children*

die Badezone, -n — *swimming area*

der Abenteuerspielplatz, ⸚e — *adventure playground*

der Babysitterdienst, -e — *baby-sitter service*

das Ausflugsprogramm, -e — *program(me) of excursions*

das Hochseeangeln — *deep sea fishing*

der Schiffsausflug, ⸚e — *boat trip*

die Sauna, -en	sauna
der Strandkorb, ⁼e	beach chair
die Segel- und Tauchschule, -n	sailing and diving school
der Reiterhof, -e	riding stables
möbliert	furnished
die Kurzreise, -n	mini-trip; short break
der Mindestaufenthalt, -e	minimum stay
der Tagespreis, -e	daily rate
die Nebenkosten, -	surcharges; extra charges
die Pauschale, -n	flat rate
Mietpreis je Woche	rent per week
die Wohneinheit, -en	accommodation unit

Seite 77   Page 77

der Traumurlaub. -e	dream holiday
ich sagte	I said
diese Hitze	this heat
wunderbar	wonderful
diese Einsamkeit	this solitude
herrlich	splendid
zurückfliegen	to fly back
Wann fliegen wir eigentlich zurück?	When actually do we fly back?
eigentlich	actually
morgen früh	tomorrow morning

Seite 78   Page 78

Zurück nach Unterschleimbach.	Back to Unterschleimbach.
die Rückfahrkarte, -n	return ticket
die Fahrkarte, -n	ticket
Und zwar zurück.	In fact, back home.
einfach	single; one-way
hin	to; towards
Einfach oder hin und zurück?	Single or return?
überhaupt	at all
Jetzt verstehe ich überhaupt nichts mehr.	Now I don't understand anything at all.
deshalb	for that reason
Deshalb fahre ich ja zurück.	That's why I am going back.
wohlfühlen	to feel at ease
Ich fühle mich hier nicht wohl.	I don't feel at ease here.

Contrastive notes

fahren (pages 68 and 69): *Fahren* is used for English *to go* when the going is done by car, by train or by ship.

an, auf, in, nach (page 68): All of these denote movement to a place.
An is used when you go to the "edge" of a place, like a beach or a riverside.
Auf is used when you climb to the top of a hill or mountain, up a tree or on to a table.
In is used when you go into a region, such as the Alps or the Ruhr district.
Nach is used with names of towns and most countries.
billiger, kleiner (page 70): In German you add the comparative ending *-er* to all adjectives, regardless of how long they are.
A number of irregular forms are listed on page 135, under *4b) Steigerungsformen.*

am besten (page 70): Where the English superlative form would be *best, cheapest, most beautiful* (or *the best* etc.), German superlative forms are combined with *am,* e. g. *am besten, am billigsten, am schönsten:*
Privatzimmer finde ich am besten.
Privatzimmer sind   am billigsten.

welcher, welche, welches, welchen (pages 72, 75 and 135): This interrogative, meaning *which,* has to correspond in gender and grammatical case to the noun concerned. This is achieved by choosing the correct ending, i. e. the ending of the appropriate article; e. g. *der Gasthof – Welcher Gasthof?* or *die Pension – Welche Pension?* or *das Hotel – Welches Hotel?*

Word order (page 134): When using verbs of movement, you usually mention the place the movement leads to. This "Direktivergänzung" always takes the position of "compulsory supplement" tinted light blue in our table. Any additional information, e. g. about the time, is placed in the green space directly in front of this: *Ich fahre morgen nach Köln.*

Lektion 7   Kursbuch

Seite 79	Page 79
das Geschenk, -e	present
das Bild, -er	picture
der Kugelschreiber, -	ballpoint pen
das Briefpapier, -	writing paper
die Tasche, -n	bag
die Kamera, -s	camera

freut Euch mit uns	*be happy with us*
heiraten	*to marry*
die Geburtstagsparty	*birthday party*
Zu unserer Geburtstagsparty laden wir ein.	*We invite you to our birthday party.*
schenken	*to give*
die Blume, -n	*flower*
Weihnachten	*Christmas*
das Jubiläum, -en	*anniversary*
Dezember	*December*

Seite 80 / Page 80

schenken	to give (s. o. sth. as a present)
Schenken macht Freude.	Giving gives pleasure.
die Freude, -n	pleasure
deshalb	therefore, so
Deshalb möchte ich ein Buch haben.	So I would like a book.
der Brief, -e	letter
rauchen	to smoke
mögen	to like, to be fond of → see contrastive notes, p. 64
der Kassettenrecorder, -	cassette recorder
die Kassette, -n	cassette
das Feuerzeug, -e	lighter
die Schallplatte, -n	record
die Zigarette, -n	cigarette
der Film (= zum fotografieren), -e	film
die Schreibmaschine, -n	typewriter
der Werkzeugkasten, ⁻	tool box
der Plattenspieler, -	record player

Seite 81 / Page 81

der Geburtstag, -e	birthday
Herr Mahlein hat Geburtstag.	It is Mr. Mahlein's birthday.
schenken	to give
Frau Mahlein schenkt ihm einen Plattenspieler.	Frau Mahlein gives him a record player.
ihm, ihr, ihnen	to him, to her, to them → see contrastive notes, p. 63
das Radio, -s	radio

58

Fred möchte ein Radio kaufen.	Fred wants to buy a radio.
erklären	to explain
Der Lehrer erklärt ihr den Dativ.	The teacher is explaining the Dative to her.
der Dativ	Dative
der Buchhändler, -	bookseller
Der Buchhändler zeigt ihnen die Bücher.	The bookseller shows them the books.
zeigen	to show
lieben	to love
Lisa liebt Jochen.	Lisa loves Jochen.
der Verkäufer, -in	salesman, salesgirl
der Verkäufer empfiehlt ihm einen Radiorecorder.	The salesman suggests a radio radio-cassette recorder.
die Platte, -n (= Schallplatte)	record
Sie kauft ihm eine Platte von Hannes Wader.	She buys him a record by Hannes Wader.
von	by
dann	then
geben	to give
Dann gibt sie ihm die Platte.	Then she gives him the record.
die Person, -en	person
reisen	to travel
gern reisen	to like travelling
die Blume, -n	flower

Seite 82   Page 82

die Party, -ies	party
Ich möchte eine Party geben.	I would like to give a party.
Hast du Lust zu kommen?	Would you like to come?
passen	to suit
Paßt es dir denn Samstag?	Would Saturday suit you?
einladen	to invite
Laden Sie diese Personen ein.	Invite these people.
diese	these
mitbringen	to bring along
Was kann ich ihm wohl mitbringen?	What on earth can I take him?
wohl	→ see contrastive notes, p. 64
der Alkohol	alcohol
Er trinkt keinen Alkohol.	He doesn't drink alcohol.
eins	one → see contrastive notes, p. 64

Er hat schon eins.	He already has one.
selten	seldom
Er liest selten.	He seldom reads.
der Aschenbecher, -	ash tray
das Wörterbuch, ⁼er	dictionary

Seite 83 / Page 83

morgen	tomorrow
Ulla hat morgen Geburtstag.	Tomorrow is Ulla's birthday.
stimmen	to be right.
Ach ja, stimmt.	Oh yes, that's right.
wissen	→ see contrastive notes, p. 64
Weißt du nicht etwas?	Can't you think of anything?
doch	→ see contrastive notes, p. 64
Schenk ihr doch eine Platte.	Give her a record.
meinen	to think
Meinst du?	Do you think so?
die Idee, '-n	idea
unpersönlich	impersonal
Das ist mir zu unpersönlich.	I find that too impersonal.
langweilig	boring
Das ist so langweilig.	That's so boring.
helfen	to help
Dann kann ich dir auch nicht helfen.	Then I cannot help you either.
das Jubiläum, ⁼en	anniversary
die Hochzeit, -en	wedding

Seite 84 / Page 84

der Toaster, -	toaster
der Topf, ⁼e	pot
der Mixer, -	mixer
zum Geburtstag	for (her/his birthday
der Pelz, -e	fur
das Mädchen, -	girl
Himmel!	Heavens!
für	for
Sie bekommen ihn für 2000 DM.	It's yours for 2000 DM.
darüber	→
Ich muß noch mal darüber nachdenken.	I shall have to think it over.
nachdenken	to think over
herzlichen Glückwunsch	(many) congratulations

hoffen
  Ich hoffe, du magst ihn.

to hope
  I hope you like it.

Seite 85 | Page 85

der Fernseher, -
welche
  Haben Sie noch welche?
darüber nachdenken
  Ich muß darüber nachdenken.
schauen
  Nein danke, ich schau nur mal.
andere
  Haben Sie noch andere?
das Sonderangebot, -e
  Hier ist ein Sonderangebot.
Den nehme ich.
die Batterie, -n

television
→
  Have you got any left?
to think it over
  I must think it over.
to look
  No thank you, I'm just looking.
others
  Have you got any others?
special offer
  Here is a special offer.
→ see contrastive notes, p. 64
battery

Seite 86 | Page 86

einpacken
  Packen Sie ihn bitte ein.

to wrap
  Please wrap it up.

Seite 87 | Page 87

die Vase, -n
  Welche Vase nehmen wir?
ausgeben
  Sie möchten nur 30.– DM ausgeben.
hübsch
  Hier ist noch eine, die ist hübscher.
bestimmt
  Die gefällt ihm bestimmt.
verschieden
  Schreiben Sie verschiedene Dialoge.
das Beispiel, -e
  Die Sätze sind nur Beispiele.
der Satz, ⁻e

vase
  Which vase shall we take?
to spend
  They only want to spend 30 DM.
pretty
  Here is another one, it's prettier.
certainly, sure
  He's bound to like it.
different
  Write different dialogues.
example
  The sentences are only examples.
sentence

die Anzeige, -n	*advertisement*
die unbegrenzte Möglichkeit	*limitless potential*
filmen	*to film*
das Gerät, -e	*instrument*
einfach	*simple*
Die Kamera ist einfach zu bedienen.	*The camera is simple to use.*
drücken	*to press*
der Auslöser, -	*release mechanism*
etwas Besonderes	*something special*
die Solarzelle, -n	*solar cell*
das Tageslicht	*daylight*
erstaunlich	*astonishing*
die Spitzentechnik, -en	*the highest technology*

Wo steht das im Text?	Where is that in the text?
über	about
Möchten Sie noch etwas über die Kamera wissen?	Would you like to know anything else about the camera?
die Foto-Messe, -n	photographic fair
Auf der Foto-Messe.	At the photographic fair.
jedes Jahr	every year
Die ist jedes Jahr in Köln.	It takes place in Cologne every year.
der Apparat, -e	camera
Können Sie mir den Apparat erklären?	Could you explain this camera to me?
funktionieren	to work
Wie funktioniert der Apparat?	How does this camera work?
die Garantie, -n	guarantee
Wie lange hat man Garantie?	How long is the guarantee?
liefern	to deliver
Wann können Sie den Apparat liefern?	When could you deliver this camera?
die Information, -en	information
Welche Informationen sind neu im Gespräch?	Which information is new in the dialogue?

Meine Damen und Herren	*Ladies and gentlemen*
technisch	*technically*
technisch perfekt	*technically perfect*

perfekt	*perfect*
einfach	*simply*
Er kann einfach alles.	*It can do simply everything.*
rechnen	*to calculate*
Er kann rechnen.	*It can calculate.*
selber	*self*
Sie selber brauchen also nicht mehr rechnen.	*So you (yourself) no longer need to calculate.*
sehen	*to see*
sogar	*even*
Er kann sogar denken.	*It can even think.*
denken	*to think*
vollkommen	*perfect*
Er ist einfach vollkommen.	*It is simply perfect.*
verlassen auf	*to rely on*
Verlassen Sie sich auf mich.	*You can rely on me.*
endlich	*at last*
Finden Sie endlich Zeit für sich selber.	*And finally have more time for yourself.*
sich selber	*yourself, yourselves*

Seite 91 / Page 91

das Glück	*happiness; luck*
kein Glück	*no luck*
möglichst am Stück	*unsliced, if possible*
das Stückchen, -	*little piece*
die Scheibe, -n	*slice*
in Scheiben	*sliced*
überhaupt	*at all*
Was haben Sie denn überhaupt?	*What <u>do</u> you have then?*

Contrastive notes

ihm, ihr, ihnen (pages 81 and 135/136): Some verbs need more than a subject and a compulsory supplement to make a complete statement. The verb *to give*, for instance, denotes an action with three components involved: somebody ("subject") gives something ("compulsory supplement") to somebody. In English, this recipient of something will be marked, grammatically speaking, either by the position in the sentence or, if put at the end, by adding *to: to Fred, to him, to me.* German, however, refers to this recipient by using a specific grammatical case, the "Dativ", bringing with it yet another set of pronouns, the forms of which are listed on page 135.

63

These pronouns show up in the sentence as "unstressed compulsory supplement" ("unbe-tonte obligatorische Ergänzung"). This supplement holds the position in front of the "addi-tional information" space; in the table on page 136, this position is tinted brown and head-ed "unbetonte obligatorische Ergänzung". However, it can also move to the front position and cause inversion (like any "Angabe" or "obligatorische Ergänzung"), e. g. *Ihr möchte ich gern Blumen schenken.* – *She is the one I'd like to give some flowers to.*

Picasso mögen (page 80): Apart from being used as a modal verb in conjunction with an infi-nitive, *mögen* can be used as a verb on its own, meaning *to be fond of.*

wohl (page 82): Germans tend to use the modifier *wohl* where in English the phrase opening *I wonder* . . . is appropriate:
Was kann ich ihm wohl mitbringen? – *I wonder what I could take him.*

eins, einen (pages 82 and 137): Used as a pronoun, the indefinite article adopts the endings of gender and grammatical case, *einer* and *einen* substituting for masculine nouns, *eins* for neuter nouns and *eine* for feminine nouns. As there is no indefinite article for plural nouns, *welche* is used as the pronoun to substitute for all indefinite plural nouns.

Schenk ihr doch eine Platte (page 83): This is another instance of a suggestion coming in the shape of an imperative softened by the modifier *doch*, as described in Lektion 4 (see the last paragraph of the entry *Nehmen Sie? Nimm!* on page 41)

wissen, kennen (page 83): A first rough-and-ready guide for making a tricky distinction: *ken-nen* is used for *to know* in the sense of *to be acquainted with* or *to have seen/read/heard (and still remember),* whereas *wissen* is *to know* in the sense of *to have learnt, to have understood* or *to have made up one's mind.*

Der ist günstig, den nehme ich. (pages 85 and 137): The accusative pronouns *ihn, sie* and *es* cannot be moved to the front position and bring about "inversion". If, for reasons of emphasis or logical connection, you want your accusative in first position, you have to use the definite article *den, die* or *das* instead of the personal pronoun.

Lektion 8 Kursbuch

Seite 93	Page 93
das Beispiel, -e	example
zum Beispiel	for example
die Hauptstadt, ¨-e	capital
der Einwohner, -	inhabitant
Die meisten Einwohner hat Hamburg.	Hamburg has most inhabitants.
interessant sein an	interesting
Und was ist noch an Hamburg interessant?	And what else is interesting about Hamburg?
das Land (= Bundesland), ¨-er	state (= federal state)
davon	→
Hamburg ist eins davon.	Hamburg is one of them.
der Bürgermeister, -	Mayor
gleichzeitig	at the same time
Der Bürgermeister ist gleichzeitig einer der 10 Ministerpräsidenten.	The mayor is at the same time one of the 10 prime ministers.
der Ministerpräsident, -en	Prime Minister
der Fluß, ¨-e	river
der Kanal, ¨-e	canal
mehr Kanäle als in Venedig	more canals than in Venice
mehr . . . als	more . . . than
die Brücke, -n	bridge
der Hafen, ¨-	port, harbour
etwa	some
Hier kommen im Jahr etwa 20 000 Schiffe an.	Some 20 000 ships come here each year.
das Schiff, -e	ship
die Tonne, -n	ton
Sie bringen 60 Millionen Tonnen Ware.	They bring 60 million tons of goods.
die Ware, -n	goods
die Pressemetropole, -n	centre of newspaper publishing
überall	everywhere; all over
Hamburger Zeitungen liest man überall in der Bundesrepublik.	Hamburg newspapers are read all over the Federal Republic.
bekannt	well known
Am bekanntesten sind:	The best known are:
das Exemplar, -e	copy
die Kulturmetropole, -n	cultural centre

das Museum, -en	museum
die Kunstgalerie, -n	art gallery
fast	almost
Hamburg hat fast 100 Kinos.	Hamburg has almost 100 cinemas.
das Problem, -e	problem
Hamburg hat auch seine Probleme.	Hamburg also has its problems.
der Schiffsverkehr	shipping
die Industrie, -n	industry
werden	to become
immer größer	→ see contrastive notes, p. 72
schmutzig	dirty
Elbe und Nordsee werden immer schmutziger.	The Elbe and the North Sea are getting dirtier and dirtier.
sterben	to die
Die Fische sterben.	Fish are dying.
langsam	slowly
Die Fischindustrie geht langsam kaputt.	The fishing industry is slowly breaking up.
kaputt gehen	to break up
die Energie, -n	energy
der Haushalt, -e	household
privat	private
weitere Atomkraftwerke	further nuclear power stations
Hamburg möchte noch weitere Atomkraftwerke bauen.	Hamburg would like to build even more nuclear power stations.
bauen	to build
wollen	to want
Viele Leute wollen keine Atomenergie.	Many people do not want nuclear energy.
die Atomenergie, -n	nuclear energy
der Bundesdeutsche, -n	West German
die Traumstadt, ⁻e	city of (their) dreams
der Senat, -e	the parliament in Hamburg

Seite 94 | Page 94

der Bus, -se	bus
die Busreisen	coach tours
die Abfahrt, -en	departure
der Erwachsene, -n	adult
der Hauptbahnhof, ⁻e	main station
über	over
die Köhlbrandbrücke über der Elbe	the Köhlbrand Bridge over the Elbe
unter	under

66

unter der Elbe	under the Elbe
mitten	in the middle
mitten in der Stadt	in the middle of the city
die Alsterarkaden	*the Alster Arcades*
an der Alster	*by the Alster*
das Wahrzeichen, -	*symbol*
das Wahrzeichen von Hamburg	*the symbol of Hamburg*
vor	in front of
vor dem Turm	in front of the tower
der Turm, ̈e	*tower*
das Denkmal, ̈er	*statue; monument*
das Bismarck-Denkmal	*the statue of Bismarck*
die Nacht, ̈e	*night*
St. Pauli bei Nacht	*St. Pauli by night*
neben	as well as
Cafés neben Kinos	Cafes as well as cinemas
der Nachtclub, -s	*night club*
das Segelboot, -e	*sailing boat*
auf	on
Segelboote auf der Alster	sailing boats on the Alster
hinter	behind
hinter ihnen:	behind them
aus dem Jahre 1842	built in 1842, dating from 1842
links	to the left
rechts	to the right
zwischen	between
zwischen den Türmen	between the towers
der Prospekt, -e	brochure
Lesen Sie den Prospekt.	Read the brochure.
zuerst	first
Wohin fährt der Bus zuerst?	Where does the bus go first?

Seite 95   Page 95

der Treffpunkt, -e	meeting point
Treffpunkt Landungsbrücken	Meeting point by the jetties.
die Brücke, -n	jetty
auf der Brücke	on the pier
der Eingang, ̈e	entrance
Oder am Eingang Brücke 3?	Or at the entrance to pier 3?
also gut	all right, then
die Sonnenuhr, -en	sundial

die Terrasse, -n	terrace
die Caféterrasse	cafe terrace
die Plattform, -en	platform

Seite 96 | ## Page 96

wo?; wohin?	→ see contrastive notes, p. 72
das Rathaus, ⁼er	City Hall
das Arbeitsamt, ⁼er	labour exchange; job centre
das Museum, -en	museum
die Geschichte, -n	history
die Kunsthalle, -n	art gallery
die Schwimmhalle, -n	indoor schwimming pool
die Öffentliche Bücherei, -en	public library
die Spielbank, -en	casino
der Sportplatz, ⁼e	sports ground
der Park, -s	park
der Markt, ⁼e	market

Seite 97 | ## Page 97

telefonieren	to telephone
Wo kann man telefonieren?	Where can I make a phone call?
leihen	to borrow
Bücher leihen	to borrow books
segeln	to sail
der Arzt, ⁼e	doctor
geradeaus	straight ahead, straight on
Sie gehen hier immer geradeaus.	Keep going straight on.
vorbei	past
an der St. Petrikirche vorbei	past St Peter's Church.
bis an	up to
bis an die Kreuzung	up to the crossing
die Kreuzung, -en	crossing
links	left
dann links	then left
rechts	right
Rechts ist das Thalia-Theater.	On the right is the Thalia Theatre.
fremd	strange
Ich bin auch fremd hier.	I am a stranger here too.

der Plan, ⁻e
    Nehmen Sie den Plan auf S. 96.

map
    Lookat the map on p. 96.

die erste
    die erste/zweite/dritte/vierte
    Straße links.

the first
    the first/second/third/fourth
    street on the left

die zweite

the second

die dritte

the third

die vierte

the fourth

die Markthalle, -n
    an der Markthalle rechts

the covered market
    turn right at the covered market

zuhören
    Nehmen Sie den Plan und hören Sie zu.

to listen
    Look at the map and listen.

der Autofahrer, -
    Der Autofahrer ist am Fernsehturm.

driver
    The driver is by the television tower.

der Fernsehturm, ⁻e

television tower

wirklich
    Wohin fährt der Autofahrer wirklich?

really
    Where is he really heading for?

die Information, -en
    Ist die Information falsch?

information
    Is the information wrong?

der Weg, -e
    Erklären Sie ihm den Weg.

way
    Tell him the way.

die Schnellbahn, -en
    Die Schnellbahnen im Hamburger
    Verkehrsverbund.

suburban railway; commuter train
    The suburban railways in Hamburg's
    integrated transport network.

der Verkehrsverbund, -e

integrated transport network

die Institution, -en

institution

das Gebäude, -

building

der Stadtteil, -e

district of a town

kommen zu
    Wie komme ich zum Rathaus?

to get to
    How do I get to the town hall?

bis zu
    Nehmen sie die S1 bis zu den
    Landungsbrücken.

as far as
    Take the S1 as far as the jetties.

U (= U-Bahn) Untergrundbahn

underground (railway); subway

umsteigen
    Steigen Sie dann in die U3
    Richtung Merkenstraße um.

to change direction
    Then change to the U3, going
    towards Merkenstraße.

die Richtung

direction

die Station, -en | station
Das ist die dritte Station. | That is the third stop.

das Tor, -e | gate
die Welt | world
  Hamburg ist das Tor der Welt. | Hamburg is the gateway to the world.
der Seehafen, ¨ | seaport
  Hamburg ist einer der größten | Hamburg is one of the largest seaports
  Seehäfen der Welt. | in the world.
sondern | but
das Meer, -e | sea, ocean
der Fluß, ¨sse | river
  Es liegt zwar nicht direkt am Meer, | It is not actually by the sea,
  sondern am Fluß. | it is on the river.
fließen | to flow
nördlich | north
  Die Elbe fließt weiter nördlich | Further north, the Elbe flows into
  in die Nordsee. | the North Sea.
das Seeschiff, -e | ocean-going ship; oceanliner
  Man kann Hamburg mit dem Seeschiff | You can reach Hamburg with ocean-
  erreichen. | going ships.
die Verbindung, -en | connection
  Es gibt gute Verbindungen nach | There are good connections to Hamburg.
  Hamburg. |
regelmäßig | regular
  Es gibt regelmäßige Schiffsverbindungen | There are regular shipping links within
  in Europa. | Europe.
die Schiffsverbindung, -en | shipping link
die Kaimauer, -n | quayside
  Viele Schiffe liegen an den Kaimauern. | Many ships are lying at the quayside.
die Hafenstadt, ¨-e | port
  Von Hamburg fahren die Schiffe | From Hamburg, ships sail to the ports
  in die Hafenstädte der Welt. | of the world.
führen | to lead
  Der Kanal führt von der Elbe durch | The canal leeds from the Elbe through
  Schleswig-Holstein. | Schleswig-Holstein.
verbinden | to link
  Der Nord-Ostseekanal verbindet | The Kiel Canal links Hamburg to
  Hamburg mit Skandinavien. | Scandinavia.
die Ware, -n | goods

70

Hamburg ist ein wichtiger Transitplatz für Waren aus der DDR, Österreich, ...	Hamburg is an important point of transshipment for goods from the GDR, Austria ...
landen	to land,
Täglich landen in Hamburg ungefähr 139 Linienflugzeuge.	Every day about 139 scheduled aircraft land in Hamburg.
täglich	daily
das Linienflugzeug, -e	scheduled aircraft
Osteuropa	Eastern Europe
Die Elbe ist eine günstige Verbindung zwischen Hamburg und Osteuropa.	The Elbe is a good link between Hamburg and Eastern Europe.
die Flugverbindung, -en	flight connection
Flugverbindungen gibt es ...	flights connecting to ...
Skandinavien	Scandinavia
Die Autobahnen nach Skandinavien führen alle über Hamburg.	The motorways to Scandinavia all go via Hamburg.
die City	city centre
Die Bahn fährt direkt in die City.	The train goes straight to the city centre.

Seite 102 / Page 102

hoffnungsvolle Auskunft	hopeful information
zuerst	first
zuerst rechts	first right
die Ampel, -n	(traffic) lights
bei der Ampel scharf rechts	sharp right at the lights
scharf	sharp
über den Platz weg	across the square
dann um das Hochhaus herum	then round the tall building
die Tankstelle, -n	petrol station
bei der Tankstelle links halten	keep to the left at the petrol station
noch einmal	again
dann fragen Sie noch einmal	then ask again
der Bogen, -	→
in einem Bogen um das Hochhaus herum	round the block of flats
wenn	if
und wenn man Ihnen sagt	and if you are told
verlieren	to lose
die Hoffnung, -en	hope
Verlieren Sie nicht die Hoffnung.	Don't give up hope.

71

Contrastive notes

immer größer (page 93): Together with the comparative of an adjective, *immer* means *more and more*, e. g. *immer größer* is *bigger and bigger, immer schmutziger* means *dirtier and dirtier, immer mehr* is simply *more and more*.

wo – wohin (pages 96/97 and 138/139): The prepositions of spatial relation listed on page 139 under. 5. *Übersicht: Wechselpräpositionen* are used with the Dativ when describing the position of somebody or something. However, when the goal of a motion is to be indicated, these same prepositions are used with the Akkusativ. The distinction rests on the verb: *sein, stehen, liegen* for instance indicate a static condition and require a "Situativergänzung" (a "positional supplement", in the dative), whereas *fahren, kommen, gehen* indicate motion towards something and require a "Direktivergänzung" (a "directional supplement", in the accusative).

zum Rathaus (pages 99 and 139): *Zu* does not follow the rule described in the previous paragraph. Although indicating a movement towards a place, it is one of those prepositions which are always followed by the Dativ. Most of these are listed on page 139 under 6. *Übersicht: Präpositionen nur mit Akkusativ oder nur mit Dativ.*

Lektion 9   Kursbuch

Seite 103	Page 103
die Gesundheit, -en	health
Gesundheit ist das höchste Gut.	Health is the greatest treasure.
tun	to do
Was tun Sie für Ihre Gesundheit?	What do you do for your health?
täglich	daily, a day
3 × täglich	three times a day
Die Stirne kühl, die Füße warm,	Cool brow and warm feet will ruin the
das macht den reichsten Doktor arm.	richest doctor.
Arzt für Allgemeinmedizin	general practitioner
Sprechst. (= Sprechstunde)	surgery hours
arbeitsunfähig	unable to work
häufig	frequent
die Ursache, -n	cause
die Erkältung, -en	cold
die Grippe	flu
das Rheuma	rheumatism

das Gelenk, -e	joint
die Bandscheibe, -n	disc
der Unfall, -̈e	accident
der Magen, -̈	stomach
der Darm, -̈e	intestine
das Herz, -en	heart
der Kreislauf, -̈e	circulation
gesund	healthy
Besser reich und gesund.	Better rich and healthy.
die Rechnung, -en	bill

Seite 104 — Page 104

die Hand, -̈e	hand
der Kopf, -̈e	head
der Arm, -e	arm
das Auge, -n	eye
die Nase, -n	nose
der Mund, -̈er	mouth
der Busen, -	bosom
der Bauch, -̈e	abdomen; stomach
das Bein, -e	leg
der Fuß, -̈e	foot
der Finger, -	finger
das Ohr, -en	ear
das Gesicht, -er	face
der Zahn, -̈e	tooth
der Hals, -̈e	neck
die Brust, -̈e	breast
der Rücken, -	back
das Knie, -e	knee
der Zeh, -en	toe
weh tun	to hurt
Mein Rücken tut weh.	My back hurts.
das Problem, -e	problem
Frau Bartels hat Probleme mit der Gesundheit.	Mrs Bartels has problems with her health.
sein Kopf – ihre Schulter	→ see contrastive notes, p. 81
jeden Tag	every day
Frau Bartels hat jeden Tag eine neue Krankheit.	Mrs Bartels has a new illness every day.
die Krankheit, -en	illness
die Schulter, -n	shoulder

Was fehlt ihm/ihr?	What is wrong with him/her?
der Schmerz, -en	pain
der Zahnschmerz, -en	toothache
Er/sie hat Zahnschmerzen.	He/she has toothache.
die Grippe	flu
Er/sie hat Grippe.	He/she has flu.
das Fieber	temperature
der Durchfall	diarrhoea
krank	ill, sick
Er/sie ist krank.	He/she is ill.
erkältet sein	to have a cold
Er/sie ist erkältet.	He/she has a cold.
grüß (→ grüßen) dich	Hello! → see contrastive notes, p. 81
Grüß dich, Gisela.	Hello, Gisela.
aussehen	to look
Du siehst aber nicht gut aus.	You really don't look well.
Was ist denn los?	What's wrong?
schlimm	bad
Ist es sehr schlimm?	Is it very bad?
ziemlich	rather; quite
Ja, ziemlich.	Yes, quite bad.

der Leser, -	*reader*
Leser fragen	*readers ask*
die Frage, -n	*question*
die Sprechstunde, -n	*surgery*
der Experte, -n	*expert*
Experten anderer Fachbereiche beraten ihn.	*Experts from other fields advise him.*
der Fachbereich, -e	*field, area, discipline*
das Gesundheitsmagazin, -e	*health magazine*
Schreiben Sie an das Gesundheitsmagazin.	*Write to the health magazine.*
die Sorge, -n	*worry*
morgens	*in the morning*
besonders morgens	*especially in the morning*
lieber	*dear*
Lieber Doktor Braun!	*Dear Dr. Braun!*
Sport treiben	*to do sport*

Ich treibe viel Sport.	*I do a lot of sport.*
sonst	otherwise
ganz	quite
Ich bin sonst ganz gesund.	*Otherwise I am quite healthy.*
gegen	→
Was kann ich gegen die Schmerzen tun?	*What can I do to stop the pains?*
gefährlich	dangerous
Ihre Schmerzen können sehr gefährlich sein.	*Your pains could be very dangerous.*
der Rat	advice
Ich kann Ihnen leider keinen Rat geben.	*I'm afraid I cannot give you any advice.*
unbedingt	definitely
müssen	must
Sie müssen unbedingt zum Arzt gehen.	You must definitely see a doctor.
das Penizillin	penicillin
sollen	shall → see contrastive notes, p. 81
Was soll ich tun?	What should I do?
recht haben	to be right
Ihr Arzt hat recht.	*Your doctor is absolutely right.*
der Streß	stress
Magenschmerzen, das heißt Streß.	*Stomach ache, that means stress.*
das Magengeschwür, -e	gastric ulcer
Vielleicht haben Sie ein Magengeschwür.	*Perhaps you have got a gastric ulcer.*
dürfen	to be allowed → see contrastive notes, p. 81
Sie dürfen keinen Kaffee trinken.	You must not drink coffee.
Sehr geehrter Herr Doktor!	*Dear Doctor!*
nervös	→
Ich bin auch sehr nervös.	*I also suffer a lot from nerves.*
wenig	little
Er sagt, ich soll weniger arbeiten.	*He said I should work less.*
wollen (→ will)	to want to → see contrastive notes, p. 81
Sie wollen keine Medikamente nehmen.	You don't want to take any medicine.
vorsichtig	careful
Dann müssen Sie aber vorsichtig leben.	*But then you really have to be careful.*
oft	often
Sie dürfen nicht oft schwimmen gehen.	*You must not go swimming (too) often.*
der Salbeitee	sage tea
Sie müssen Salbeitee trinken.	*You must drink sage tea.*
die Halskompresse, -n	throat compress

Sie müssen jeden Abend Hals- kompressen machen.	You must make a throat compress every night.

Seite 107 — Page 107

der Ratschlag, ⁓e	advice
Welche Ratschläge gibt Dr. Braun?	What advice does Dr. Braun give?
die Tablette, -n	tablet
Sie brauchen Magentabletten.	You need stomach tablets.
ein paar Tage	a few days
Sie müssen erstmal ein paar Tage ins Bett.	First you must stay in bed for a few days.
abends	in the evening → see contrastive notes, p.81
Diese Tabletten nehmen sie abends.	Take these tablets in the evening.
mittags	mid-day; noon → see contrastive notes, p. 81
Das nehmen Sie mittags.	Take this around mid-day.
morgens	in the morning → see contrastive notes, p. 81
Das nehmen Sie morgens.	This you take in the morning.

Seite 108 — Page 108

sogar	→
Oh ja, das soll ich sogar.	Oh yes, in fact I'm supposed to.
die Schokolade, -n	chocolate
die Verstopfung, -en	constipation
zu dick sein	to be too fat
die Fischallergie, -n	allergy to fish
die Herzbeschwerden	a heart complaint, heart trouble
besuchen	to visit
Sein Freund Rolf besucht ihn.	His friend Rolf visits him.
die Fußballmannschaft, -en	football team
ein wichtiges Spiel	an important match
denn	because
Seine Mannschaft braucht ihn, denn er spielt sehr gut.	His team needs him, because he plays very well.
unbedingt	definitely
mitspielen	to play too
Du mußt unbedingt mitspielen.	You really must play, too.
bestimmt	surely

90 Minuten kannst du bestimmt spielen.	You can surely play 90 minutes.
bleiben	stay
Ich will im Bett bleiben.	I want to stay in bed.
doch	→
Spiel doch mit!	Do play!
wichtig	important
Meine Gesundheit ist mir wichtiger als das Spiel.	My health means more to me than the match.
wirklich	really
Kannst du wirklich nicht?	You really can't?
dann nicht	in that case, no
Na gut, dann nicht.	Well then, in that case, no.
wünschen	to wish
Ich wünsche dir gute Besserung.	I wish you a speedy recovery.

Seite 109	Page 109
der Nachbar, -n	neighbour
Schreiben Sie weitere Dialoge mit Ihren Nachbarn.	Write further dialogues with your neighbours.
die Jazzband, -s	jazz band
die Trompete, -n	trumpet
Roland spielt in einer Jazzband Trompete	Roland plays the trumpet in a jazz band.
das Wochenende, -n	weekend
Am Wochenende müssen sie spielen.	They have to play at the weekend.
die Firma, -men	firm; company
Herr Koch arbeitet bei der Firma Heinen KG.	Mr. Koch works for the firm of Heinen KG.
seit	since; for
Er ist seit 10 Tagen (letzter Woche) krank.	He has been ill for ten days (since last week).
der Chef, -s	boss
anrufen	to phone
Sein Chef ruft ihn an.	His boss phones him.
eventuell	*perhaps*
die Arbeitsunfähigkeitsbescheinigung	*sick note*
die Bescheinigung, -en	*certificate*
Der Arzt schreibt ihm dann eventuell eine Arbeitsunfähigkeitsbescheinigung.	*Then the doctor may perhaps write him out a sick note.*
der Arbeitnehmer, -	*employee*

der Arbeitgeber, -	*employer*
Die Bescheinigung gibt der Arbeitnehmer dem Arbeitgeber.	*The employee gives the certificate to his employer.*
kündigen	*to dismiss; to give notice*
Der Arbeitgeber darf dem Arbeitnehmer dann nicht kündigen.	*The employer is not allowed to dismiss the employee.*
der Lohn, ⁻e	*wage*
weiterzahlen	*to continue paying*
Der Arbeitgeber muß den Lohn für sechs Wochen weiterzahlen.	*The employer must continue paying the wages for six weeks.*
Name des Versicherten	*name (of insured)*
die Erstbescheinigung, -en	*first certification*
die Folgebescheinigung, -en	*further certification*
vorlegen	*to present; to give*
Bitte sofort dem Arbeitgeber vorlegen.	*Please give to your employer immediately.*
der Arbeitsunfall, ⁻e	*accident at work, industrial accident*
die Arbeitsunfallfolge, -n	*consequence of a work-related accident*

Seite 110	Page 110
Mensch, was hast du denn gemacht?	Hey, what have you done?
bloß	→
Was ist denn bloß passiert?	What on earth happened?
passieren	to happen
erzählen	to tell
Erzähl mal!	Tell me!
ordnen	to arrange
Ordnen Sie die Bilder.	Arrange the pictures.
die Geschichte, -n	story
Es gibt drei Geschichten.	There are three stories.
nach unten	to take downstairs
Ich habe die Bierflaschen nach unten gebracht.	I was taking the bottles of beer downstairs.
der Kollegin, -nen	colleague, workmate (m; f)
Meine Kollegin ist gekommen und hat mir geholfen.	A colleague of mine came and helped me.
fallen	to fall
Dann bin ich gefallen.	Then I fell.

Seite 111   Page 111

plötzlich	suddenly
Plötzlich ist meine Hand in die Maschine gekommen.	Suddenly my hand got into the machine.
brechen	to break
Das Bein ist gebrochen.	The leg is broken.
schreien	to cry out
Da habe ich laut geschrieen.	Then I cried out.
wie immer	as usual
Ich habe wie immer an der Maschine gearbeitet.	I was working at the machine as usual.

Seite 112   Page 112

Ski fahren	skiing
Hartmut hat in Bayern Ski fahren gelernt.	Hartmut learned to ski in Bavaria.
der Skikurs, -e	ski(ing) course
Der Skikurs hat 3 Wochen gedauert.	The skiing course lasted three weeks.
täglich	daily
Hier das tägliche Programm.	Here the daily program(me).
das Programm, -e	program(me)
der Anfänger, -	*beginner*
Der Skikurs Anfänger	*The ski course for beginners*
das Skitraining	*ski training*
der Januar	January
Der 30. Januar war ein Unglückstag.	The 30th January was a bad day.
der Unglückstag, -e	terrible day (day of accidents); misfortune, disaster

Seite 113   Page 113

der eingebildete Kranke	*the hypochondriac*
gesund	*healthy*
glauben	*to believe, to think*
Glauben Sie, ich bin krank?	*Do you think I'm ill?*
Mein Gott!	*Good heavens!*
irgend etwas	*something*
Irgend etwas tut mir nicht weh.	*Something doesn't hurt.*
bis jetzt	*so far*
Bis jetzt noch nicht.	*Not so far.*

der Unsinn	nonsense
die Verdauung	digestion
Wie ist Ihre Verdauung?	How is your digestion?
gar nicht	not at all
Nicht gut – gar nicht gut!	Not good – not at all good.
verdauen	to digest
Sie verdauen schlecht!	You digest badly!
mit einem Wort	in a word
Mit einem Wort, Ihre Verdauung ist schlecht.	In a word, your digestion is bad.
der Schluß	end
Jetzt ist aber Schluß.	Cut it out now.
der Appetit	appetite
Sie haben keinen Appetit.	You have no appetite.
gerade	just
Aber Sie sagen doch gerade . . .	But you said just now . . .
die Niere, -n	kidney
Was ist mit Ihren Nieren?	How about your kidneys?
funktionieren	to function
der Punkt, -e	point
Das ist auch so ein Punkt.	That's a point, too.
manchmal	sometimes
Manchmal frage ich mich: Hast du überhaupt Nieren?	Sometimes I ask myself, have you any kidneys at all?
überhaupt	at all
jeder Mensch	everybody
sicher	sure
Sind Sie ganz sicher?	Are you quite sure?
wahrscheinlich	probably
Wahrscheinlich trinken Sie auch zu wenig.	You are probably drinking too little.
vor allem	above all
Ich trinke Bier, Limonade und vor allem Wasser.	I drink beer, lemonade and, above all, water.
ausschwitzen	to sweat out
Ich glaube, ich schwitze alles wieder aus.	I think I sweat it all out.
laufen	to run
Ich laufe ständig zum Arzt.	I keep running to the doctor.
ständig	constantly
die Konsultation, -en	consultation
Für die Konsultation: fünfzig Mark!	For the consultation, 50 Mark!

Contrastive notes

sein Kopf, ihre Schulter (pages 104 and 140): The "possessive articles" *sein, ihr* etc. (you will find a complete list on page 140 under *1. Possessivartikel*) take the same endings as the indefinite articles *ein* and *eine*.

Grüß dich, Gisela. (page 105): *Grüß dich.* and *Grüß Gott.* are southern German equivalents of *Guten Tag.* Of course, *Grüß dich.* is appropriate only where there is a "du"-relationship.

dürfen, sollen, wollen (pages 106 and 140): These are three further modal verbs. Like *möchte* (cf. the note on page 23), they are used with the infinitive of another verb and take the first verb position in the sentence, the infinitive verb going to the second verb position at the end.

morgens, mittags, abends (page 107): These can be used to indicate that something happens usually or regularly at those times of the day.

Sie müssen ins Bett. (page 107): Used as a verb on its own, *müssen* takes a "Direktivergänzung" ("directional supplement") and carries the meaning *one has got to go somewhere.*

Perfect (pages 110 and 141): On page 141 you will find, under *a) Formen*, the past participles of some verbs. In German, the "Perfekt" is used for actions that have been completed, but not for actions or circumstances that are still going on; for those, the present tense is used and marked accordingly with a modifier, most often *schon.* Thus, the English sentence *He has been ill for ten days*, would be rendered in German by *Er ist schon seit zehn Tagen krank.*

Some German verbs take the auxiliary verb *sein* rather than *haben*; generally speaking, they are those verbs which denote either a change of place or a change of modality. Seven of these are listed on page 141. On the same page, under *b) Präsens und Perfekt im Satz,* the position of each element of the verb in the sentence is shown: the auxiliary, *haben* or *sein*, in the first verb position and the past participle in the second verb position at the end of the sentence. You may want to compare this with the modal verbs shown on page 140.

Seite 114

die Friedensdemonstration, -en	*peace demonstration*
der Krieg, -e	*war*
die Arbeitslosigkeit	*unemployment*
die Eltern (Pl.)	*parents*
die Fußballweltmeisterschaft, -en	*football World Cup*

Page 114

Seite 115

werden
  Italien ist Fußballweltmeister
  geworden.
sterben
  Ingrid Bergman ist gestorben.
der Friede
  In New York haben 500 000
  Menschen für den Frieden
  demonstriert.
demonstrieren
sie hatten
  Millionen Menschen hatten keine
  Arbeit.
heiraten
lieben
der Besen, -
  Ich habe zwei neue Besen gekauft.

to become
  Italy became the world champion in
  football.
to die
  Ingrid Bergman died.
peace
  In New York, 500.000 people
  demonstrated for peace.
to demonstrate
they had → see contrastive notes, p. 89
  Millions of people had no work.
to marry
to love
broom
  I bought two new brooms.

Seite 116

eigentlich
  Wo warst du eigentlich Montag?

du warst
verabreden
  Wir waren doch verabredet.
total
  Das habe ich total vergessen.
vergessen

actually, really
  Where were you actually on Monday
  evening?
you were
to make an appointment; to have a date.
  We did have a date.
totally
  I totally forgot about it.
to forget

ich war	I was
Da war ich im Kino.	I was in the cinema.
morgen	morning
Montag morgen	Monday morning
mittag	mid-day, lunchtime
Dienstag mittag	Tuesday lunchtime
nachmittag	afternoon
Donnerstag nachmittag	Thursday afternoon
abend	evening
Samstag abend	Saturday evening
gestern	yesterday
Was hast du gestern abend gemacht?	What did you do yesterday evening?
die Giftsuppe, -n	*poison soup*
Ich habe eine neue Giftsuppe gekocht	*I made a new poison soup.*
die ganze Zeit	all this time
Was hast du denn die ganze Zeit gemacht?	What have you been doing all this time?

Seite 117 | ## Page 117

die Arbeiterdemonstration, -en	*workers' demonstration*
die Schulklasse, -n	*class*
Schwarzer Freitag	*Black Friday*
das Geld	*money*
Die Menschen haben wenig Geld.	*People have little money.*
die Polizei	*police*
Die Polizei bringt viele Menschen ins Gefängnis.	*The police arrest many people.*
das Gefängnis, -se	*prison*
die Weltwirtschaftskrise, -n	*The Great Depression; The World Depression*
Die Weltwirtschaftskrise fängt an.	*The Great Depression begins.*
die Koalition, -en	*coalition*
Eine Koalition ist an der Regierung.	*A coalition is in power.*
an der Regierung sein	*to be in power/government*
der Reichskanzler	*Reich Chancellor*

Zeittafel Seite 118/119 | ## Chronological table pages 118/119

die Weimarer Republik	*Weimar Republic*
demokratisch	*democratic*

Die erste demokratische Republik zerfällt nach und nach.	The first democratic republic gradually collapses.
der Arbeitslose, -n	unemployed
der Führer, -	Führer, leader
der Jude, -n	Jew
verlieren	to lose
Die deutschen Juden verlieren die bürgerlichen und politischen Rechte.	German Jews lose civil and political rights.
die bürgerlichen und politischen Rechte	civil and political rights
die Schulden	debts
Deutschland hat Schulden.	Germany has debts.
die Milliarde, -n	thousand million
die Militärparade, -n	military parade

Zeittafel Seite 120/121

Chronological table pages 120/121

der Weltkrieg, -e	World War
töten	to kill
In Deutschland töten die Nazis ...	In Germany the Nazis kill ...
der Nazi, -s	Nazi (National Socialist)
der geistig und physisch Behinderte	mentally and physically handicapped person
der psychisch Kranke	psychologically disturbed person
verfolgen	to persecute
In Polen verfolgt Hitler besonders die polnische Intelligenz.	In Poland, Hitler persecutes especially the Polish intelligentsia.
die Intelligenz	intelligentsia
Osteuropa	Eastern Europe
Krieg erklären	to declare war
Hitler erklärt den Krieg.	Hitler declares war.
die Endlösung der Judenfrage	the Final Solution of the Jewish Question
ermorden	to murder
Bis 1945 ermorden Hitler und seine Helfer ungefähr ...	By 1945, Hitler and his helpers had murdered about ...
der Zigeuner, -	gipsy
mehrere Hunderttausend	many hundred thousand
das Attentat, -e	(attempted) assassination
ohne Erfolg	unsuccessful
Ende des 2. Weltkrieges	end of the 2nd World War

Seite 118

Page 118

der Vater, -̈	father

der Kriegsinvalide, -n	*war disabled*
die Schule, -n	school
das Abitur	*Abitur (German school leaving examination); diploma*
der Soldat, -en	*soldier*
Soldat in Westpreußen	*soldier in West Prussia*
Westpreußen	*West Prussia*
das Theologiestudium	*theological studies*
der Religionslehrer, -	*teacher of Religious Education*
Religionslehrer in München.	*RE teacher in Munich.*
damals	*at that time*
Wie haben Sie die Zeit damals erlebt?	*How did you experience those times?*
leicht	easy
Wir hatten es nicht leicht.	We did not have it easy.
nämlich	→ see contrastive notes, p. 89
Mein Vater war nämlich Kriegs- invalide.	You see, my father was disabled in the war.
schon	certainly
Ja, das kann man schon sagen.	Yes, you could certainly say that.
Wie ist das gekommen?	How did that come about?
bis 1941	till 1941
das Gymnasium	*high school*
Ich bin dann zum Gymnasium gegangen.	*Then I went to the high school.*

Seite 119	**Page 119**
der Sozialdemokrat, -en	*Social Democrat*
der Elektriker, -	*electrician*
ernst	*serious*
Ich war damals sehr ernst.	*I was very serious then.*
nachts	*at night*
Nachts hat er Flugblätter geschrieben.	*At night he wrote pamphlets.*
das Flugblatt, ̈-er	*pamphlet*
verteilen	*to distribute*
Seine Freunde haben die Flugblätter dann verteilt.	*His friends distributed the pamphlets.*
die Gestapo	*the Gestapo (Hitler's secret police)*
In der Nacht ist die Gestapo gekommen.	*At night, the Gestapo came.*
nach	*after*
nach drei Tagen	*after three days*
vorsichtig	*careful*

Aber er war dann sehr vorsichtig.   *But then he was very careful.*
anders   *different*
Unser Lehrer Wimmer war dann anders.   *Our teacher Wimmer was different.*

Seite 120   Page 120

das Studium   *studies*
1946 habe ich dann mein Studium angefangen.   *Then in 1946 I began my studies.*
denken   *to think*
Was haben Sie über Hitler gedacht?   *What did you think about Hitler?*
jung   *young*
Ich war noch jung.   *I was still young.*
verteidigen   *te defend*
Wir müssen Deutschland verteidigen.   *We must defend Germany.*
im Krieg fallen   *to be killed in action*
Viele sind im Krieg gefallen.   *Many were killed in action during the war.*
die Zeit   *time*
Die Zeit war sehr schlimm.   *Times were bad.*
kaputt   *finished*
Sehen Sie, 1945 war Deutschland kaputt.   *You see, in 1945 Germany was finished.*
tot   *dead*
Millionen von Menschen waren tot.   *Millions of people were dead.*
der Anfang, ⁻e   *beginning*
Ich habe einen neuen Anfang gesucht.   *I looked for a new beginning.*

Seite 121   Page 121

einmal   *once*
Einmal ist er in die Schule gekommen.   *Once he came into school.*
Heil Hitler!   *Heil Hitler!*
lachen   *to laugh*
Wir haben gelacht.   *We laughed.*
darauf   *at that*
Darauf hat er geantwortet ...   *At that he answered ...*
der Bube, -n (südd.) (= der Junge)   *boy (South German)*
das Massengrab, ⁻er   *mass grave*
Deutschland geht jetzt ins Massengrab.   *Germany is now heading for a mass grave.*
der Kommunist, -en   *Commmunist*
Unser Lehrer ist ein Kommunist.   *Our teacher is a Communist.*
Setzen Sie ein!   Fill in.

der Lebenslauf, ̈e	*curriculum vitae*
Er studiert Jura.	*He studies Law.*
bestehen	*to pass*
Er besteht das Juraexamen.	*He passes his (final) exam in law.*
die Staatsanwaltschaft, -en	*public prosecutor's (Am: District Attorney's) office*
das Gericht, -e	*court*
Er arbeitet beim Gericht.	*He works at the law courts.*
der Assistent, -en	*assistant*
der Rechtsanwalt, ̈e	*lawyer*
Er ist Assistent bei einem Kölner Rechtsanwalt.	*He works as an assistant to a Cologne lawyer.*
das Mitglied, -er	*member*
der Beigeordnete, -n	*deputy mayor*
der Bürgermeister, -	*mayor*
der Oberbürgermeister, -	*Lord Mayor*
entlassen	*to dismiss*
Er wird entlassen.	*He is dismissed.*
ziehen nach	*to move to*
Er zieht mit seiner Familie nach Rhöndorf.	*He moves with his family to Rhöndorf.*
verhaften	*to arrest*
Er wird von der Gestapo verhaftet.	*He is arrested by the Gestapo.*
der Vorsitzende, -n	*Chairman*
der Bundeskanzler, -	*Federal Chancellor*
die Arbeiterpartei, -en	*Worker's Party*
die Schiffsmaklerfirma, -firmen	*firm of shipbrokers*
illegal	*illegal*
Er schreibt illegal Flugblätter gegen die Nazis.	*He writes pamphlets illegally against the Nazis.*
fliehen	*to flee*
Er flieht nach Norwegen.	*He escapes to Norway.*
ändern	*to change*
Er ändert seinen Namen.	*He changes his name.*
organisieren	*to organise*
das Ausland	*foreign country*
der Widerstand, ̈e	*resistance*
Er organisiert im Ausland den Widerstand gegen Hitler.	*He organises the resistance to Hitler abroad.*
die Staatsbürgerschaft, -en	*citizenship*
Er verliert die deutsche Staatsbürgerschaft.	*He loses German citizenship.*

überfallen	to attack
Hitler überfällt Norwegen.	Hitler attacks Norway.
das Exil, -e	exile
Er wird Mitglied der Exil-SPD.	He becomes a member of the SPD in exile.
die Scheidung, -en	divorce
der Abgeordnete, -n	parliamentary deputy
der Bundestag, -e	West German federal parliament
regierender Oberbürgermeister	Governing Mayor
Bundeskanzlerkandidat, -en	Candidate for the Federal Chancellorship
der Friedensnobelpreis, -e	Nobel Peace Prize
Er bekommt den Friedensnobelpreis.	He receives the Nobel Peace Prize.

Seite 123	Page 123
abgeschlossene Vergangenheit	completed past
H-J (= Hitler Jugend)	Hitler Youth
der Text, -e	text
Ach, das ist so ein Text.	Oh, it's just a text.
der Geschichtslehrer, -	history teacher
Den Text hat uns der Geschichts- lehrer gegeben.	Our history teacher gave us the text.
die Jugend	young people
direkt	exactly
So direkt kann man das nicht sagen.	It isn't exactly like that.
singen	to sing
Wir haben viel gesungen.	We sang a lot.
marschieren	to march
Wir sind viel marschiert.	We marched a lot.
Disco, -s	disco
Discos hat es damals noch nicht gegeben.	There were no discos in those days.
die Schulaufgabe, -n	homework
Was ist mit deinen Schulaufgaben?	How about your homework?
fertig	finished
Bist du fertig?	Have you finished?
fast	almost
der Junge, -n	boy
Fast alle Jungen waren damals ...	Almost all the boys were at that time ...
Mein Gott!	Heavens!
noch anderes	other things too
Wir haben auch noch anderes gemacht.	We did other things, too.
das Lagerfeuer, -	camp fire

Lagerfeuer und so.	*Camp fires, that sort of thing.*
genau	exactly, precisely
Warum willst du das eigentlich so genau wissen?	*Why do you want to know it so precisely?*
der Opa, -s	grandpa
also nicht richtig	not exactly
vorbei	past
Das ist alles schon lange vorbei.	*That's all long since past.*
endlich	at last; finally
Jetzt mach endlich deine Schulaufgaben.	*Come on and do your homework now.*

Contrastive notes

hatten, war (page 115): The perfect tense of the verbs *haben* and *sein* is usually avoided in German, preference being given to the <u>past tense</u> of these two verbs.

nämlich (page 119): *Nämlich* is roughly equivalent to English *you see*; it marks the sentence in which it stands as being the explanation for what may have been left unresolved or puzzling in a preceding sentence. In this instance, the statement *Das war schlimm für meine Familie.* provokes the unspoken question, *What was the matter with his family?* The word *nämlich* in the following phrase makes it clear that that sentence is intended as an answer to that unspoken question.

Lektion 1 Arbeitsbuch

Lektion 2 Arbeitsbuch

Ausland, Seite 20	Export edition, page 20
ohne	without
ohne Namen	without a name
der Traum, ⸚e	dream
nicht wissen	not to know
nicht wissen wo	not to know where

kauen	to chew
lutschen	to suck
Silben zum Kauen und Lutschen	syllables to chew and suck
die Brieffreundschaft, -en	pen friendship
hübsch	pretty
Ich bin ganz hübsch.	I am quite pretty.
der Rentner, -	pensioner

Inland, Seite 20/21   Home edition, page 20/21

das Telefonhäuschen, -	telephone kiosk
verschieden	different
die Münze, -n	coin
das Gespräch, -e	call
der Selbstwähldienst, -e	STD (subscriber trunk dialling)
besetzt	engaged
verwählt	mis-dialled
die Taste, -n	button
grün	green
die Postkarte, -n	postcard
der Brief, -e	letter

Lektion 3   Arbeitsbuch

Ausland, Seite 29   Export edition, page 29

der Turm, ⸚e	tower
der Bahnhof, ⸚e	station
Kunst studieren	to study art
im Erdgeschoß (das Erdgeschoß)	on the ground floor
im 5. Stock (der 5. Stock)	on the 5th floor

Seite 30   Page 30

eine eigene Wohnung	one's own home
Junge Leute möchten eine eigene Wohnung.	Young people want their own home.
das Programm, -e	programme
ein Möbelprogramm für junge Leute	a furniture range for young people

Inland, Seite 29 | Home edition, page 29

das Problem, -e
problem

Typisch ist die Konzentration in
den Großstädten.
Typical is the large number of
foreigners in the cities.

die Arbeit
work

Denn hier gibt es Arbeit.
Because here, there is work.

anonym
unnoticed

Wir möchten gern anonym leben.
We should like to live unnoticed.

der Garten, ∹
garden

die Natur
nature

Denn es gibt keinen Garten und
keine Natur.
Because there is no garden and
no nature.

isoliert
isolated

Wir sind isoliert.
We are isolated.

der Mieter, -
tenant

Seite 30 | Page 30

bieten
to offer

Biete 2-Zimmer-Wohnung.
2-room flat offered.

die Anzeige, -n
small ad

Das kostet eine Anzeige
(in der Zeitung).
That takes a small ad
(in the newspaper).

tragen
to carry

die Last
burden

Die einen tragen des andern Last.
Some carry another's burden.

der Vermieter, -
landlord

Lektion 4 Arbeitsbuch

Ausland, Seite 39 | Export edition, page 39

gesund
healthy

Das ist gesund.
That is healthy.

viel
a lot

Sie essen sehr viel.
They eat a lot.

der Lastwagenfahrer, -
lorry driver, truck driver

das Müsli
muesli

Morgens esse ich immer ein Müsli.
In the morning I always have
some muesli.

91

eine Diät machen	to go on a diet
wenig Zeit	little time
Morgens haben wir immer nur wenig Zeit.	In the mornings we always have little time.
der Hunger	hunger
Ich habe keinen Hunger.	I am not hungry.

Seite 40 — Page 40

lieben	to love
Ein bißchen Liebe	A little love
der Schmerz, -en	pain
das Glück	happiness
Ein bißchen Glück	A little happiness
Nichts besonderes	nothing special
Liedchen aus alter Zeit	song from old times
die Sardine, -n	sardine
die Olive, -n	olive
der Retsina	retsina (Greek wine)
vergessen	to forget
Haben Sie den Krieg ganz vergessen?	Have you quite forgotten the war?
Neulich stand in der Zeitung.	Recently it said in the paper.
gefangene politische Gegner	captured political opponents
gefoltert	tortured
der Honig	honey
in Not (die Not)	in need
Manche Kinder sind in Not.	Many children are in need.
der Früchtequark	fruit flavoured quarg (rather like curds)
stark machen	to make strong
Früchtequark macht stark.	Fruit quarg makes you strong.
die Götterspeise	ambrosia, food of the gods
das Leibgericht, -e	favourite meal
tot	dead
Manche Kinder sind schon tot.	Many children are already dead.

Inland, Seite 39 — Home edition, page 39

einfach	simple
Die griechische Küche ist sehr einfach.	Greek cooking is very simple.
gleich	the same
Die Speisekarten in den Restaurants sind gleich.	The menus in the restaurants are the same.

die Portion, -en	portion
Man bekommt hier große Portionen.	You get large portions here.
freundlich	friendly
Der Service ist sehr freundlich.	The service is very friendly.
der Preis, -e	price
Hier sind nur die Preise hoch.	Here only the prices are high.
das Nudelgericht, -e	spaghetti dish, noodles
die Phantasie	imagination
Hier kocht man ohne Phantasie.	The cooking is unimaginative.
am Hafen (der Hafen)	by the docks
sitzen	to sit
Man sitzt dort sehr gemütlich.	It is very cosy there.
das Geflügelgericht, -e	poultry
unter 30 Mark	less than 30 Mark
Alle Hauptgerichte kosten	All main courses cost
unter 30 Mark.	less than 30 Mark.
nach dem Essen (das Essen)	after the meal

Seite 40	Page 40
einkaufen	to go shopping
alles	everything
Wir bekommen meistens alles.	We usually get everything.
der Supermarkt, ¨-e	supermarket
das Kaufhaus, ¨-er	department store
das Spezialitätengeschäft, -e	delicatessen
die Lebensmittel (Pl.)	food
das Gewürz, -e	spice
die Apotheke, -n	chemist
das Maismehl	Indian meal, corn meal

Lektion 5 Arbeitsbuch

Ausland, Seite 51	Export edition, page 51
die Freizeit	leisure time
das Angebot, -e	offer
Die Freizeitindustrie hat	The leisure industry always has
immer neue Angebote.	something new to offer.
das Mitglied, -er	member
faul	lazy

Das ist ein Club für faule Freizeit.	That is a club for lazy leisure time.
weit	far
Die Fahrt ist zu weit.	The journey is too far.
der Fehler, -	mistake
Ist das ein Fehler?	Is this a mistake?
allein sein	to be alone
manchmal	sometimes
fast	almost
Sie sind fast ein Faulenzergenie.	You are almost a genius at being lazy.
nervös	tense
Sie sind zu nervös.	You are too tensed up.

Seite 52 / Page 52

weniger	less
mehr	more
die Weiterbildung	further education
Weniger arbeiten, mehr Zeit haben für die Weiterbildung – das möchten viele.	To work less, to have more time for further education – many would like that.
so weiß man aus Umfragen	that one knows from surveys
die Teilzeitstelle, -n	part-time job
der Arbeitnehmer, -	employee
teilen	to share
Zwei Arbeitnehmer teilen sich eine Arbeitsstelle.	Two employees share a job between them.
das Gehalt, -̈er	salary
der Arbeitgeber, -	employer
die Gewerkschaft, -en	trade union
der Arbeitslose, -n	unemployed

Seite 53 / Page 53

Was meinen Kinder dazu?	What do children think of this?
liebhaben	to love
Ich habe meine Mutter sehr lieb.	I love my mother a lot.
helfen	to help
müde	tired

Inland, Seite 51 / Home edition, page 51

die Kasse	box office

Karten an der Konzertkasse	Tickets at the concert box office
täglich	daily
schnarchen	to snore

Seite 52/53

Page 52/53

die Freizeit	leisure time
der Erwachsene, -n	adult
der Landkreis, -e	district
das Kursangebot, -e	range of courses
die Naturwissenschaft, -en	science
die Kunst	art
die Sprache, -n	language
berufskundliche Fächer	vocational subjects
Es gibt Kurse für Naturwissenschaften, Kunst, Sprachen und berufskundliche Fächer.	There are courses for sciences, art, languages and vocational subjects.
der Anmeldetermin, -e	enrolment date
geschlossen	closed
Im Sommer ist die Schule geschlossen.	In summer the college is closed.
die Kenntnisse	knowledge

Lektion 6 Arbeitsbuch

Ausland, Seite 63

Export edition, page 63

der Nörgler, -	grouser
der Pechvogel, ⸚	born loser
der Alleswisser, -	know-all
der tolle Hecht	gay dog
der Reiseleiter, die Reiseleiterin	courier; tour guide
unzufrieden	dissatisfied
der Regen	rain
der Koffer, -	suitcase
verlieren	to lose
Der Pechvogel verliert immer etwas.	The born loser is always losing something.
die Zahnschmerzen	toothache
seit 10 Jahren	for the last ten years
betrunken sein	to be drunk
pünktlich sein	to be punctual

95

böse sein
　Alle mögen ihn, niemand ist
　wirklich böse.

to be angry
　Everybody likes him, nobody is
　really angry.

Seite 64　　　　　　　　　　　Page 64

der Urlaub — holiday
tauschen — to exchange
　Die Familien tauschen jedes Jahr
　ihre Wohnungen.
　The families exchange their homes
　every year.
dieses Jahr — this year
letztes Jahr — last year
das Abenteuer, - — adventure
der Massenurlaub — mass tourism
wenig bekannte Gebiete (das Gebiet) — less known areas
　Viele Menschen möchten lieber in
　wenig bekannte Gebiete reisen.
　Many people prefer to go to less
　known areas.
organisiert sein — to be organised
　Auch die Abenteuerreisen sind
　schon organisiert.
　Even the adventure trips
　are organised.
die Wüste, -n — desert
der Urwald, ⁻er — jungle
planen — to plan
der Strand, ⁻e — beach
im Frühjahr (das Frühjahr) — in spring
im Herbst (der Herbst) — in autumn

Inland, Seite 63　　　　　　Home edition, page 63

der Tramper, - — hitch-hiker
leicht — easy
Spaß machen — to be fun
　Trampen ist leicht und macht Spaß.
　Hitch-hiking is easy and fun.
geöffnet — open
　Die Raststätten haben Tag und Nacht
　geöffnet.
　The services are open day and night.
nett — nice
sauber — clean
das Gepäck — luggage
　Du mußt nett und sauber aussehen
　und nicht viel Gepäck haben.
　You must look nice and clean
　and not have too much luggage.
der Lastwagenfahrer — lorry driver

halten	to stop
Der Fahrer hält.	The driver stops.
die Landschaft, -en	scenery
die Straßenkarte, -n	road map
die Jugendherberge, -n	youth hostel

Seite 64	Page 64
die Rückfahrkarte, -n	return ticket
der Geltungstag, -e	day of validity
Man muß am 1. Geltungstag abfahren.	You must start your journey on the first day of validity.
die Hinfahrt, -en	outward journey
die Rückfahrt, -en	return journey
beliebig	as one likes
unterbrechen	to interrupt
Man kann die Fahrt beliebig unterbrechen.	You can break your journey as you wish.

Lektion 7 Arbeitsbuch

Ausland, Seite 72	Export edition, page 72
schließen	to close
Die Geschäfte schließen.	Shops are closing down.
die Lebensmittel	food
der Supermarkt, ⁻e	supermarket
die Bedienung	service
der Besitzer, -	owner
das Schuhgeschäft, -e	shoe shop
der Friseur	hairdresser's
der Modeladen, ⁻	boutique
die Versicherung, -en	insurance agency
früher	earlier

Seite 73	Page 73
Geld ausgeben	to spend money
die Abteilung, -en	department
die Süßigkeit, -en	sweet
das Getränk, -e	drink

der Wunschzettel, -	request list
Weihnachten	Christmas
Bei dir piept's wohl?	Have you gone mad?
die Forderung, -en	demand
das Gegenangebot, -e	counter-proposal
verhandeln	to bargain

Inland, Seite 72/73 — Home edition, pages 72/73

der Gebrauchtwagen, -	second hand car
der Führerschein, -e	driving licence
verlieren	to lose
Man verliert beim Verkauf viel Geld.	You lose a lot when you sell it.
der Händler, -	dealer
wert sein	to be worth
auf dem Land (das Land)	in the country

Seite 74 — Page 74

das Gerät, -e	set, piece of equipment
der Produzent, -en	manufacturer
die Garantiebedingung, -en	guarantee condition
reparieren	to repair
der Preisunterschied, -e	price difference
vergleichen	to compare
Man muß die Preise vergleichen.	You must compare prices.
das Sonderangebot, -e	special offer

Lektion 8 Arbeitsbuch

Ausland, Seite 85 — Export edition, page 85

bauen	to build
bleiben	to remain
Sauerlach muß ein Dorf bleiben.	Sauerlach must remain a village.
das Gemeindeparlament, -e	village council; municipal council
selten	rarely

Seite 86	Page 86
krank	diseased
die Bürgerinitiative, -n	action committee
kämpfen	to fight
sauber	clean
Bürgerinitiativen kämpfen für einen sauberen Fluß.	Action committees are fighting for a clean river.
bekannt	known
Viele bekannte Gruppen spielen hier.	Many well-known groups play here.
die Veranstaltung, -en	meeting
einen guten Geschmack haben	to have good taste
der Liedermacher, -	chansonnier, folk singer
die Kleinkunst	cabaret

Inland, Seite 85	Home edition, page 85
der Parkplatz, ¨e	parking place
das Benzin	petrol
der Dauerparker, -	long-term parker
der Kurzparkplatz, ¨	short-term parking place
P + R (= park and ride)	park and ride
kostenlos	free
die Plakette, -n	sticker
pünktlich	punctual
regelmäßig	regular
die Tarifzone, -n	fare zone
das Verkehrsnetz	traffic network

Seite 86	Page 86
die Behörde, -n	authority
der Wegweiser, -	signpost
die Versicherung, -en	insurance
die KFZ-Zulassungsstelle, -n	vehicle licensing office
prüfen lassen	to have checked
ummelden	to change the registration (In Germany this includes a new number plate.)
abmelden	to end the registration.

Lektion 9 Arbeitsbuch

Ausland, Seite 97

die Mehrheit, -en	majority
die Lösung, -en	solution
Gegen Durchfall hilft eine	A salt and sugar solution
Salz-Zucker-Lösung.	is good for diarrhoea.
gefährlich	dangerous
der Todesfall, ⁓e	case of death
die Bakterien	bacteria
die Darmflora	intestinal flora

Export edition, page 97

Seite 98/99

das Gold	gold
Angst haben	to be afraid
das Einkommen	income
streiken	to strike
Sie haben Angst um ihr Einkommen	They are anxious about their incomes
und wollen streiken.	and want to strike.
durchschnittlich	on average
verdienen	to earn
das Kostendämpfungsgesetz, -e	Cost Reduction Act
der Gummikopf, ⁓e	rubber head
das Metall, -e	metal
die Brücke, -n (= die Zahnbrücke)	bridge
einer raus	one comes out
einer rein	one goes in
selber rein	(go) in myself

Page 98/99

Inland, Seite 97

prakt. (= praktische) Ärztin	general practitioner
das Medikament, -e	medicine
die Tablette, -n	tablet
die Therapie, -n	treatment
die Zusammensetzung, -en	contents
das Anwendungsgebiet, -e	application
die Gegenanzeige, -n	side effects
der Warnhinweis, -e	warning

Home edition, page 97

die Dosierungsanleitung, -en	dosage instructions
die Art der Anwendung	method of use
unzugänglich für Kinder aufbewahren	keep out of the reach of children

Seite 98/99	Page 98/99
das Gehalt, ⁻er	salary
die Not	need; misery
Die Not ist sehr groß.	Misery is widespread.
die Untersuchung, -en	examination
die Behandlung, -en	treatment
die Brille, -en	spectacles
der Arbeitnehmer, -	employee
der Arbeitgeber, -	employer
Den Arzt darf man frei wählen.	You have a free choice of doctor.
das Honorar, -e	fee
das Mitglied, -er	member

Lektion 10 Arbeitsbuch

Ausland, Seite 106	Export edition, page 106
die Propaganda	propaganda
der Widerstand, ⁻e	resistance
das Flugblatt, ⁻er	pamphlet
schicken	to send
Sie schicken Flugblätter in andere Städte.	They send pamphlets to other towns.
die Vorlesung, -en	lecture
verbreiten	to distribute
Sie können die Flugblätter verbreiten.	They can distribute the pamphlets.
der Innenhof der Universität	the inner courtyard of the university
verurteilen	to sentence
sterben	to die
Der Führer befiehlt: Glauben, gehorchen und kämpfen!	The Führer commands: Believe, obey and fight!

Seite 108	Page 108
erzählen	to tell
wiest eingerückt bist	how you joined up

101

(= wie du eingerückt bist)
wiest gschossen hast   how you shot
  (= wie du geschossen hast)
wiest verwundt wordn bist   how you were wounded
  (= wie du verwundet worden bist)
wiest gfallen bist   how you were killed in action
  (= wie du gefallen bist)

Inland, Seite 106/107 — Home edition, page 106/107

der Zirkus, -se	circus
die Katze, -n	cat
die Ratte, -n	rat
die Ente, -n	duck
der Hahn, ⸚e	cockerel
der Hund, -e	dog
die Vorstellung, -en	performance
Eine Vorstellung im Zirkus Maus	A Zirkus Maus performance
dauert nicht lange.	does not last long.
der Hut, ⸚e	hat
das Tier, -e	animal
sensibel	sensitive
konsequent	consistent
der Pelzmantel, ⸚	fur coat
der Plan, ⸚e	plan

Seite 108 — Page 108

der Urlaub	holiday
der Judenstern, -e	Star of David
die Deportation, -en	deportation
Angst haben	to be afraid
verboten	forbidden
der Pfarrer, -	pastor
der Bunker, -	bunker
in Zivil	in civvies
sich verstecken	to hide

Hören Sie mal!

A program for understanding spoken German

This program provides listening practice for each of the ten units of Themen 1. The focus is on real, everyday German as it is actually spoken by native speakers.

The package consists of three cassettes and a book. The cassettes offer a large number of recordings with examples of different types of spoken language and regional varieties. The accompanying exercise book provides tasks for each recording that help students recognize the most important points and guide them, gradually step by step, to understand more clearly and in more detail what is being said. As they work through the program students discover that they have acquired the skills and strategies to understand even "difficult" texts. A transcription of the recordings and a key to the exercises is also included.

Hören Sie mal!

A Listening Comprehension program
by Claudia Hümmler-Hille and Eduard von Jan
Hueber-Nr. 1484

sprachen der welt
hueber Max Hueber Verlag · Ismaning